THE FACT OF CHRIST

THE
FACT OF CHRIST

A Series of Lectures

BY

P. CARNEGIE SIMPSON, M.A.
MINISTER OF RENFIELD CHURCH, GLASGOW

NEW YORK   CHICAGO   TORONTO
Fleming H. Revell Company
Publishers of Evangelical Literature

To my Wife

PREFATORY NOTE

THESE lectures were given in Renfield Church during last winter to a public class which met on Sunday evenings after service; they are now published without further elaboration either of matter or style. A few sentences and two or three notes have been added.

The subject has been treated strictly within certain limits, and many aspects of it have been purposely left untouched. In particular, the inquiry has been carried on as an individual question, and little or no account has been taken of the way in which religion comes to us through the Christian society and tradition, or of the way in which it must express itself in the social life of the world. The whole range of topics that are suggested by the ideas of 'Church' and 'Kingdom of God,' which are certainly parts of the meaning of Christ, are not included in the scope of this volume. Another occasion may be found for their discussion.

In passing the lectures through the press, I have tried to acknowledge and verify all quotations and references, and ask indulgence if anything in this respect has been omitted.

P. C. S.

GLASGOW,
   October 1900.

CONTENTS

I
	PAGE
THE DATA OF CHRISTIANITY	13

II
| WHAT IS THE FACT OF CHRIST? . . . . | 39 |

III
THE FIRST MEANING OF THE FACT . . .	65
I. The Christian Character	71
II. The Moral Motive-Power . . .	81

IV
THE FURTHER MEANING OF THE FACT . . .	103
I. The Foundation of Faith	106
II. 'And the Word was God' . . .	126

V

	PAGE
THE FINAL MEANING OF THE FACT . . .	141
I. The Reality of Sin	146
II. The Problem of Forgiveness . . .	157
Addendum: The Principles of the Atonement	174

VI

WHAT IS A CHRISTIAN?	191

I

THE DATA OF CHRISTIANITY.

'Christus ist nicht der Lehrer wie man zu sagen pflegt, Christus nicht der Stifter; er ist der Inhalt des Christenthums.' SCHELLING.

I

THE DATA OF CHRISTIANITY

WHEN the greatest religious Master whom the world has ever known put one day to His first disciples a certain question, and, on receiving an answer to it, declared that on the strength of this He could build His Church, it is evident that here is to be found what He regarded as the critical issue for religion and its proper point of departure. To state the religious problem as Jesus stated it is surely the most hopeful way of approaching the subject not only of Christianity, but also of religion generally, on which He is the indisputably supreme authority.

It surprises us, however, when we look at what this question was. The occasion referred to is, of course, the scene near Cæsarea Philippi, when Jesus asked His disciples, ' Whom say ye that I am? ' The question is a notable one, but it astonishes us that it should be treated as a fundamental one. The inherent truth of a teacher's message would always appear to be a more important matter than anything, however interesting, about the teacher himself. We should therefore expect that the question which Jesus would regard as of decisive importance for religion would be about some cardinal theological belief—such as: Do you believe in the Father in heaven?—or some primary ethical principle, such as: Do you accept the law of the Sermon on the Mount? This is what we should expect. But the question was not of this kind. It was not about God nor about morals. It was a question simply about Jesus Himself. It was neither theological nor ethical, but personal. And this was the question upon an answer to which Jesus declared, with energy and enthusiasm, that His Church would be built. The fact is a very remarkable one, and we cannot too carefully impress its significance upon our minds. This greatest of religious teachers forms His religion—for the building of His Church cannot be less than that—from His followers' convictions regarding Himself. What appears to be an irrelevancy to religion—the personality of the preacher—He makes its very root. It is to put the same thing in other words to say that Jesus directed men to find the data for Christianity primarily and essentially in the phenomenon of Himself.

If such a statement seem to need further evidence than a single incident, that evidence is not far to seek. It is found in the whole of the didactic method of Jesus, which was such as no other religious teacher has ever adopted. That, according to the records, the strikingly distinctive thing about the way Jesus taught and trained His followers is that He so persistently and energetically presented Himself to them is a thesis that is now almost a commonplace in any trustworthy discussion of the subject. It strikes even the casual reader of the Gospels; all the more will it do so if he compares with the manner and method of Jesus as a teacher, the manner and method of Moses or Isaiah or John the Baptist, or if he opens his Plato or the Koran. All other great teachers are profoundly conscious that they are but pointing to a realm of truth, and—all the more if they are truly great teachers—they efface themselves before its eternal principles. Alone, absolutely alone, among leaders of the soul, Jesus absorbs the highest principles into His own personality. To the seeker after eternal life He said, 'Follow Me'; of one who would see the Father, He asked, 'Hast thou not known Me?' No other teacher has ever dared thus. Who else has said of truth, not that he teaches it, but that it is he; of the vision of God, not that he has found it, but that it is in the sight of himself; of that which supplies all man's need of rest, of spiritual food, of strength, of pardon, not that he can point to it, but that it is all in him? Not Moses so spake nor the prophets; not Plato nor the Buddha nor Mahomet. But Jesus spoke thus. He did so habitually, deliberately pronouncedly. There is no doubt about this, and it differentiates Him as a teacher from all other teachers. Others know they are but messengers of truth; He is also the message. They are but torchbearers; He called Himself 'the Light of the world.' They point to truth; He said, 'Come unto Me.'

All this is the unique note of Jesus' teaching. In His training of His disciples we see it carried on systematically and step by step so distinctly that an intelligent reader perceives that the conversation at Cæsarea Philippi was not incidental, but a carefully planned climax, and therefore its result so gladly welcomed a consummation.

So Jesus, who came to preach religion, deliberately and distinctly did so by making men 'think of' Himself. As a German author of insight says, 'He knew no more sacred task than to point men to His own person.'[1] He came not to elaborate a system of theology or ethics, but to introduce Himself to men's minds and hearts, and left men with the question, not, 'What think ye of this doctrine or that principle?' but, 'What think ye of Christ?' And this means that, as has been said, Jesus directs us to find the data for Christianity primarily and essentially in the phenomenon of Himself, not in His ideas, His teaching, His example merely, but in the fact of Christ. To quote an-

[1] Herrmann's *Der Verkehr des Christen mit Gott*, Eng. trans., p. 76.

other eminent German authority—one of the most careful of examiners and a critic unbiased towards orthodoxy—Keim, after saying that 'the religion of Christ goes mysteriously back to His person,' adds, 'this fundamental fact alone enables us to understand the religion which sprang from it.'[1] To understand Christianity then is, in at least the first place, to 'think of' Christ—to say how our mind and heart and conscience regard Him. The philosophical mind, especially in the period known as the *Aufklärung,* discusses Christianity, Jesus apart, as the manifestation of eternal truths of the reason; and that, no doubt, it is. The modern, practical mind discusses it mainly as a moral motive and ideal; and these, too, doubtless, it is. But these were not the ways in which Jesus bade men approach the subject. His direction to any one who would consider the problem of religion was, in effect if not always literally, the question of Cæsarea Philippi. And, be it remembered, He is the greatest Master of religion that the world has known.

Now here is nothing less than a revolution

[1] *Jesu von Nazara,* i. 448.

in the whole study of the problem of religion. That problem, which bewilders and baffles the quest of the human spirit that is ever athirst for God, is here restated in terms which we can hardly believe to be sufficient because they are so simple. This restatement has never been sufficiently regarded, considering the authority of its source; certainly it never more needed to be regarded than to-day.

There are two notable and significant features in the condition of the question of religion at present, one on either side of the question. On the one side, unbelief has very markedly settled down into agnosticism. On the other side, Christendom, more perhaps than ever, is confused and contradictory as to what Christianity most simply and essentially is. A slight survey of these features will, I think, show that both of them have, at least in part, arisen because we have not approached the discussion of Christianity as its Author directed us to do.

Unbelief has, in our day, settled down into agnosticism. We are no longer in the days of Voltaire. We are no longer in the days even of the Deists, and hardly any one reads now Shaftesbury or Toland or Bolingbroke. Nor, if we are to have a religion at all, is there at present any serious rival to Christianity. Vagaries such as Neo-Buddhism make conversation rather than converts. But these facts do not mean that the age is agreeing to Christian faith. They mean rather a more settled refusal of it. An opposition that contended, however fiercely, that Christianity was false might always possibly be overcome; but an unbelief which submits, however courteously, that Christianity is futile, because the whole topic of religion is beyond human ken, is a far subtler foe. It is the latter which is the mental mood of very many in our time. They do not virulently deny; in many cases they long to believe. But they are agnostic; that is, they do not know. No one surely knows. Religious faith is no more than it was in Socrates' days—a thing of 'fair hopes.' It all seems far away, uncertain, unknown and probably unknowable. I am referring not so much to any philosophical statement of agnosticism, but rather to the general uncertain attitude towards religion of many a thinking man and woman. Among such, a mental attitude of this kind is very often to be found, and one serious thing about it is that with the generality of people, and despite not a few notable examples to the contrary, where religious faith becomes a mere perhaps, moral strenuousness is in danger of becoming a counsel of perfection.

But what is the reason of this uncertainty, this agnosticism? The reason is just that men more than ever feel the difficulty, the impossibility of answering at all the great questions of God and the soul. The origin and meaning of the universe are something so far and vast, and life is something so complex, that we cannot say much about them on the religious side. Nature we can know, but, though Nature stretches out to the Infinite, we cannot see what meets her there. The battle of faith and unbelief—Bishop Butler or Paley notwithstanding—was always an inconclusive one, and now less than ever are men able to take as decided in the affirmative the problems of God, of revelation, of freedom, of immortality. These questions are beyond us. Who knows? And the more serious read their Herbert Spencer and make their agnosticism a philosophy, the more shallow their Omar Khayyam and make it a pleasure, and many, many a seeking soul is left unsatisfied.

Now to every such an one—be his agnosticism intellectually self-satisfied, sensually self-indulgent, or neither of these, but only sad—comes the great Master of the soul with His revolutionary restatement of the problem of religion. What He says, in effect, is this. You say you cannot answer the great question of God: it is beyond your ken. Well, here is the way in which to approach this question; what is your attitude towards Me? Now, whatever else this question may be, it is at least this—it is answerable. Your agnosticism cannot apply here. If the being of God is beyond your ken, the fact of Christ is not. He is a fact of history, cognizable as any other phenomenon. And your mental and moral conclusions on this answerable question are the true beginnings of an answer to the apparently inscrutable problem of religion.

Thus does Jesus so restate the religious prob-

THE DATA OF CHRISTIANITY

lem as to make it at least answerable. He calls it from the region of the inscrutable to that of the positive. This is the practical answer of Christianity, as Jesus presented it, to agnosticism. The late G. H. Lewes in his *History of Philosophy* dismisses religion from the realm of verifiable knowledge because 'it confesses its inability to furnish knowledge with any available data.'[1] With the Christian religion, according to the method of Jesus, the reverse is the case. He furnished His followers with the most patent and accessible of data—the person standing before them. The data of His religion were and are in a positive fact. What are the data? Unverifiable sentiments or ideas in the inscrutable region of faith? Not so. 'Whom say ye that I am?' 'What think ye of Christ?' 'I am the truth.' 'Come unto Me.' Here are the data of Christianity. They are in an historical person, a fact as available as any other fact. Jesus drove agnosticism into the open when He declared that the data of religion are in the fact of Christ.

[1] Vol. i. p. 17.

Of course it does not necessarily or immediately follow that by driving it into the open He has defeated it. Even a fair and honest facing of the fact of Christ *may* not be sufficient to take us to a religious faith. That, of course, remains to be seen. But one may just now ask this: how many of those who assume an agnostic attitude about religion have tested this method? I mean how many of them have honestly brought their minds and hearts and consciences face to face with the fact of Christ, and candidly considered if it means anything to them for religion? It is impossible to say that no one has the right to be an agnostic. But no one has the right to be an agnostic till he thus dealt with the question—the certainly answerable question—which Jesus regarded as the critical issue and the true starting point in the matter of religion. Let us not give up— if we are in earnest we shall not give up—the great question of religion without being quite sure that there is no help to be got from the method of the great Master of religion. If an agnostic would be honest, he must spend some serious days at Cæsarea Philippi; after that, he may be an agnostic—if he can.

If the method of Jesus in stating the problem of religion has thus a direct bearing on the agnostic tendency which is one marked feature of the mind of the day, not less direct is its bearing on the other. To believe it is not the only difficulty about Christianity to a present day inquirer; the other and almost greater difficulty is to discover it. For Christendom is full of Christianities, and to say what simply and essentially is the Christian religion is one of the problems of the nineteenth Christian century. The evidence of this is manifold; it appears alike within and without the pale of the Church.

Looking without that pale, we cannot fail to be struck with this feature in the most serious and influential modern criticism of Christianity—that it is, or at least professes to be, not destructive but reconstructive. It desires not the ruin of Christianity, but its rescue. It comes not to destroy, but to deliver. It would give us the true and simple and pure Christian religion in place of the beclouded and corrupt tradition of the centuries. Christianity, it declares, has yet to be born, or at least must be born again; criticism comes not to follow its obsequies but to attend its rebirth, for at its first birth it was strangled in its cradle. In this spirit and with this aim, so their authors assure us, are written—to name two popular examples—*Literature and Dogma* and *Robert Elsmere*.

I hope it may be said without offense that to one with any grave historical sense there is something about this that savors a little of what might be described as intellectual *nouvelle richesse*. To propose to take down the structure of a Christianity that has stood for centuries, and to rebuild it largely anew, to allege that the main idea of the thing has been radically misconstrued, and needs to be stated afresh, to say that the lines laid down and followed by St. John and St. Paul, by Athanasius, Augustine, Luther, are largely misleading and a new direction must at this hour of the day be taken—one cannot help feeling that all this, like the philosophy of a man who has struck oil, lacks historic background. Under what a melancholy mistake have these nineteen centuries been laboring! On what a false scent those apostles put us! We are all *déraillés*—we are off the rails! What a pity that St. John, ' who was so much more metaphysical than his Master,' was ever allowed to write about Him, or that St. Paul, whom the older rationalism held to be the ' real creator of Christianity,' appeared just at the critical formative moment he did in Christian history! And how thankful *we* should be that now, at last, such a clever and still ingenuous man as the author of *Literature and Dogma* has come to put them and us right, and that such a gifted—and one must add, most earnest—lady as the writer of *Robert Elsmere* has shown us, in so unquestionably interesting and also eminently convenient a way, how the old construction of Christianity is (in fiction) so helpless after half an hour of squire-archical talk, and the new is (in fiction) so regenerating a power in East London. These reconstructions have many aspects of value, for the Church is constantly in danger of being a slave to its past and of thinking that a quotation from a Father or a confession is the final word of truth. But it does not do to put a fool's cap on the history of the Christian religion.

Nevertheless, the popularity which attends reconstructions of Christianity that thus profess to give us the simple and true reading of it, is very significant. It is significant of an uncertainty as to what Christianity is and how far the traditional version of it is to be trusted as genuine. This is a marked feature of the mind of our time, which, in many quarters, is much disposed to echo the well-known *dictum* that the Christian religion has now been tried for eighteen centuries but the religion of Christ remains to be tried. Much of the most popular religious criticism of the day is just the attempt to give us, in its simplest and purest form, an answer to the question: What is the religion of Christ?

The difficulty of answering this question does not appear to be lessened—it appears rather to be increased—when we pass from without to within the ecclesiastical pale. The inquirer is now bewildered by variant voices. That the world has been divided into two camps on the indubitably difficult question of whether Christianity be true is not wonderful; what is wonderful is that the professed Christian authorities have been divided into sects and schools upon the apparently simple question of what Christianity is. It is bound up, in one view of it, with an ecclesiastical rite, in another with a dogmatic belief, in a third with the morality of a man's conduct, and in yet a fourth with his inward experiences of faith and a 'new birth.' One director will ask you about your baptism, another about your conversion; this one will speak exclusively of the death of Jesus, that one of your own life. Nor do these various guides of the soul agree to regard their views as all different aspects of one truth. On the contrary, of active purpose and in express terms, will they exclude each other. 'He that believeth not shall be condemned'—the anathema, though usually in less direct language, is as familiar as its application is varied. Believeth not what? The authority of the Church, the necessity of the sacraments, the assertions of the creeds, the doctrine of the Atonement, the need of regeneration by the Spirit, the all-importance of moral life? In the household of Christians and about the simplest essentials of Christianity arises a strife of tongues to not only the confusion of truth, but also, not seldom, the extinction of charity.

And nowhere does this appear more significantly than in the great and enduring conflict between faith and unbelief. Here in the face of the common foe, one might expect that Christians could agree upon a method of attack and concentrate upon the really vital points of defense. It is far from being so. One section is ever accusing the other of imperiling the kernel with the husk, and, in turn, is accused by the other of sacrificing everything by surrendering the shell. Does Christianity go if the infallibility of the Church goes, or the inerrancy of the Bible; if the dogmas of the creed go, or miracles, or the 'doctrines of grace'? Christendom answers 'Yes' and answers also 'No.' It is all very perplexing to plain-minded men who, in the din of battle, never are sure whether they need to tremble for the ark of God or not; and it is not less exasperating to zealous opponents of Christian belief to be so often told that some point which they have assailed with all their energies is not even within the real field of battle. The result is

'Confused alarms of struggle and flight,
Where ignorant armies clash by night.'[1]

False issues, vain victories and defeats—what examples of these are to be found in the records of the Christian controversy! Sometimes it may have been, intellectually or otherwise, magnificent; often it has been miserable. But it is not war. It is not the war between truth and error, light and darkness, faith and unbelief.

In all this confusion, the voice of Jesus, as He asks the question of Cæsarea Philippi, falls on our ears with peculiar significance. Amid all your reconstructions and all your versions, He seems to say, here is *the* question. What do you say of Me? What is your attitude to Me? Criticism must not banish nor the Church bury these issues. If you would find Christianity, find it in Me—in what I am and mean to your mind and heart and conscience. So Jesus seems to speak to us. The direction is

[1] Matthew Arnold, *Dover Beach.*

surely, for every reason, to be followed. It is from the ultimate authority, for I do not imagine that any one proposes to reconstruct the Christianity of Jesus: it appeals to us distinctly and directly: it is full of intellectual and moral interest. And thus the Master whose restatement of the problem of religion makes it to the agnostic answerable, makes it also, by the same means, to the inquirer clear—clear, that is to say, not indeed in the sense of easily fathomable, but in that of being neither misconceived nor confused. The inquirer knows at least his data and can begin. He knows where Christianity is, if not yet what it is; or, to put it at the least, he knows where was its spring. Unsatisfied, perplexed, perhaps even repelled by the many Christianities he finds around him, he can 'lift up his eyes unto the hills' where Christianity took its rise. It took its rise not in a philosophic school, theological or ethical, not in an ecclesiastical system, not in a social or political proposal. It took its rise in men being brought face to face with a certain phenomenon—the fact of the person of Jesus Christ. There, indubitably, are the original data of Christianity. Whatever may be said of the building, there is the authentic site.

The first business in any inquiry is to determine your data. It appears, then that according to Jesus, the data of Christianity are to be sought for in the fact of Himself. If we would follow His method, we must begin there. We must not start from theological ideas or ethical precepts, but from a fact—the fact of Christ. We must examine what that fact is, and what it means. This is the way of rightly, clearly and simply learning Christianity and the way, at the same time, of attacking the problem of religion itself. The data of Christianity are in the fact of Christ.

In words, this may appear to be satisfactory enough. But an obvious reflection occurs to our minds and seems to invalidate its whole religious value. Is not this fact of Christ a fact of nineteen hundred years ago? Possibly to those who stood before Him, Jesus presented Himself in the way that has been indicated and thereby was of immediate religious significance to them. But how can it be identically so with us to-day? What truly and properly religious value for us is there in a figure, however wonderful, of centuries past? It is present, living truths of the spirit that religion demands. Such truths may be in the teaching of Jesus, and there therefore may be data for religion. But is this insistence on the fact of Jesus Himself really religious? How can religion, which is other than historical and theological or ethical opinion, find its data there? It may be our misfortune, but is it not an inevitable misfortune, that *we* cannot—even if the first disciples could and did—base our religion thus? To examine this fact of Christ may lead us to historical and other conclusions; but to religion—how? The data of religion can be only the eternal truths of spiritual life present and living in the soul.

The question thus raised—which finds its most authoritative expression in the opinion so frequently insisted upon by Hegel, that the content of Christianity is to be manifested by philosophy and not by history—is one we cannot and need not here discuss at length. At present we are concerned with it only as regards this point: does the fact of Christ being (as of course it is) one of past history prevent it from containing to the mind and heart and conscience that examine it, real data for religion? Well, let us see. Let us not prejudge this. We know the original site; let us examine for ourselves whether or not for us it is still available. The original site of Christianity is the fact of Christ. What is this fact of Christ?

To some, even this question may seem valueless—so intricately is it involved in philosophical presuppositions and party prejudice. The mists of controversy may appear to have settled too densely on the Galilean hills. Let us not be deterred easily by these difficulties. Let us not so despair of what a plain intelligence and an honest will can still find about this great fact. We shall at least try this. 'The question whether anything can be known,' says a master among those that know, 'is to be settled not by arguing but by trying.'[1]

[1] Bacon's *Nov. Org., præfatio.*

II

WHAT IS THE FACT OF CHRIST?

'Auctor nominis ejus Christus Tiberio imperitante per procuratorem Pontium Pilatum supplicio affectus erat.'
TACITUS.

II

WHAT IS THE FACT OF CHRIST?

JESUS CHRIST is, beyond all reasonable question, the greatest man who ever lived. The greatness of a man is to be estimated by two things: first, by the extent of his influence upon mankind; and, secondly,—for no one is altogether great who is not also good—by the purity and dignity of his character. Tried by both these tests, Jesus is supreme among men. He is at once the most influential and the best of mankind.

We are concerned at present with the fact of Jesus Himself, with therefore the latter rather than the former of the two qualities just named. We are concerned with His character rather than what He has done. As to the unparalleled impression that He has made on human life and history, I shall content myself by quoting a weighty sentence from Mr.

Lecky's *History of European Morals*. The 'three short years' of the active life of Jesus have, says Mr. Lecky, 'done more to regenerate and to soften mankind than all the disquisitions of philosophers and all the exhortations of moralists.'[1] If this statement be true —and who will dispute it?—then the secular, historical greatness is unparalleled of the man whom a Roman historian dismissed in a sentence and a Greek satirist with a sneer.[2]

Not less emphatically was He the supreme man in the realm of moral character. It were an easy task to compare Him in this respect with any other saint or hero of history and show He was morally better. To do this would be, however, but to say the least part of the truth about the character of Jesus. Let us state the complete truth at once. He had not simply less sin and more virtue than others. His supremacy is not comparative. It is absolute. Jesus is the stainless man, the one sinless human being.

[1] Vol. ii. p. 9.
[2] *Vide* the quotation from Tacitus *(Annales,* i. 15, 44) prefixed to this lecture. Lucian *(De Morte Peregrini,* xi.) calls Jesus μέγας ironically.

To prove a negative is always difficult; to prove it absolutely often an impossibility. It is obviously an impossibility absolutely to demonstrate that the life and character of any man are entirely stainless. But in the case of Jesus the witness is as strong as the very nature of the thing to be proved can possibly admit. His enemies are witnesses to it. With all their ingenuity of hate and malice, never once did they dare to prefer against Him any moral charge, and insinuations such as that 'this man receiveth sinners and eateth with them' fell harmless upon Him. His friends are witnesses. They described Him as 'separate from sinners.' They were orthodox Jews, steeped in the doctrine that 'there is none righteous, no, not one.' But they were compelled to contradict themselves. 'Yes, one,' they said against their scriptures; '*He* did no sin.' And we too are witnesses of the stainless perfection of the character of Jesus. For His friends have given us about Him far more than a vague eulogy. They have given us accounts, short indeed but particularized, of His life. They do not merely affirm His stainlessness, which were easy.

They exhibit it, which it were simply impossible to do except from the life. We have there what Jesus said and did in all kinds of circumstances and on all manner of occasions—in public and private, in the sunshine of success and the gloom of failure, in the houses of His friends and in face of His foes, in life and in the last great trial of death. It is the detailed picture of a man who never made a false step, never said the word that ought not to have been said, never, in short, fell below perfection. Such a portrait is of necessity a true portrait. It simply cannot be an idealized picture. That which is so above human criticism is not less above our conception. 'It is no use,' says the sane and acute J. S. Mill, 'to say that Christ as exhibited in the Gospels is not historical, and that we know not how much of what is admirable has been superadded by the traditions of His followers.'[1] It is no use because, as Mill goes on to ask, who among His disciples or their proselytes—who, he might have asked, among the poets and dramatists of the world? —is 'capable of inventing the sayings ascribed

[1] *Three Essays on Religion*, p. 353.

WHAT IS THE FACT? 43

to Jesus or of imagining the life and character revealed in the Gospels?'[1] Artistic inspiration is a fine thing; but it is simply nonsense—' it is no use '—to say that it reached such an unheard-of height in four Jewish writers of the first century as to enable them, and all of them harmoniously, to draw from their imaginations the lines and colors, the lights and shades of the life of the perfect man. But they did it. Only one thing accounts for their being able to do it. That is simply veracity. They had a model and they copied it faithfully. And because, first, the model was faultless, the reproduction, being faithful, was perfect too.

Our inquiry, then, as to what Jesus was receives its first emphatic and astounding answer in an assertion of something that He was not. He was not a sinner. And this at once introduces and explains to us that mysterious aloneness in Jesus by which He who was the friend and brother of the humblest is, nevertheless, in another category from the best and greatest. The difficulty of realizing the true place of Jesus among men is that of bringing

[1] *Three Essays on Religion*, p. 353.

Him into actual comparison with them, for He has impressed the imagination, not only to a degree, but also in a way that no other man has done. Instinctively we do not class Him with others. When one reads His name in a list beginning with Confucius and ending with Goethe we feel it is an offense less against orthodoxy than against decency. Jesus is not one of the group of the world's great. Talk about Alexander the Great and Charles the Great and Napoleon the Great if you will. Jesus was—as has been said, from even the secular point of view—incomparably greater than any of these; yet, who would speak of Jesus the Great? Jesus is apart. He is not the Great: He is the Only. He is simply Jesus. Nothing could add to that.

This aloneness of Jesus appears in two ways, or, rather, has two degrees. First, His whole manner betrays that His moral experience and that of other men were not parallel. He who so searchingly told others of the evil within their hearts made no confession for Himself. He who gave the despairing sinner every other token of brotherhood, never spoke as if He

Himself had been in the same case. He who was so morally sensitive that He has become the supreme conscience of mankind, yet challenged men to convict Him of sin. All this reveals a singularness by which He is not only 'separate from sinners,' but is also distinct from the saints. The saints among men all tell us how they reached sanctity, if at all, only from below, having toiled with tears and prayers up the bitter path of repentance to a newness of life. The Psalms tell us that, and the *Confessions,* and the *De Imitatione;* the whole company of holy and humble men of heart tell us that. But Jesus never tells us that.

And this is not all. There is a second thing about this strange moral aloneness of Jesus— something, not negative, but positive. Not only did Jesus never betray a sense of any moral imperfection or moral need, but, further, He regarded Himself as the sufficer of all others' need. This was referred to in the last lecture; it needs no elaboration, for it can hardly be denied, and the most labored exposition of it cannot be more expressive than the simplest statement. Listen to this voice: 'If any man thirst, let him come unto Me and drink'; 'Come unto Me, all ye that labor and are heavy laden, and I will give you rest.' The quotations suffice. They reveal one who not only is Himself without moral distress, but can aid all distress. Others are lost sheep; He is not only not lost, but is the shepherd. Others are sick; He is not only in health, but is the physician. Others' lives are forfeit; His is not only His own, but is the ransom. Others—all others—are sinners; He not only is not a sinner, but is a Saviour.

These are things that cannot but impress profoundly every candid and earnest mind. There is nothing else like them in the whole range of human nature. And they are not exaggerated dogmas of orthodoxy; they are conclusions of the most modern criticism. The most remarkable feature of religious scholarship in recent times is the study of the Jesus of nineteen hundred years ago. In the Christian centuries His personal figure had been largely lost sight of and His human face hid behind the clouds of mystic devotion or the drapings of dogma. In the Romish church Jesus was the vision of a fair face whose painful beauty won the wistful adoration of the rapt religious, but whose living form, as He was in Galilee, was hardly seen in the daylight of thought and life; to the Protestant He was too easily an official personage, the executor of certain functions, rather than the Son of Man. From both of these have men in our day turned to ask, with a new earnestness, in the name, not only, nor perhaps even mainly, of religion, but of history, the old demand: 'We would see *Jesus.*' The demand has had a remarkable response. The historical spirit, which during the past half century has profoundly influenced almost every department of knowledge, has affected none more markedly than the study of Christianity, and, in particular, of the life and character and person of Jesus. Biographies of Jesus have appeared in great numbers, written from all points of view; critical research has been lavished on every historical aspect of the question; His teaching, work, career, and personality have been studied and appreciated as never before. The result, it is not too much to say, is that Jesus who lived in Palestine is better—that is, more distinctly and more critically—known to our age than He has been known to any age since His own. And what has been the effect of all this? The effect has been that never was the wonderful, strange, and mysterious loneliness of Jesus more admitted. To modern criticism Jesus is indubitably and emphatically a phenomenon unique. As an illustration of this one may name the great work of Keim,[1] where his irresistible sense of the transcendence of his subject is ever straining to the utmost and even bursting the limits of naturalistic presuppositions. There is found about Jesus what there is about no other, and the more accurately and critically we know Him the more profoundly we feel it. He is beyond our analyses. He confounds our canons of human nature. He compels our criticism to overleap itself. He awes our spirits. There is a saying of Charles Lamb, which is responded to by a very deep feeling within the heart of every really serious student of the person of Jesus, that 'if Shakespere was to come

[1] *Geschichte Jesu von Nazara.* (English translation.)

WHAT IS THE FACT?

into this room we should all rise up to meet him, but if that person was to come into it, we should all fall down and try to kiss the hem of His garment.'[1]

Yet, despite all that has been said—which it would be easy to elaborate along the same lines, but that is unnecessary—have we found in it any real answer to the question we wish to determine? The character of Jesus may have been stainless, and His personality may be mysteriously alone among the phenomena of human nature. He may have been apparently above the otherwise universal moral needs of men, and even able to supply the needs of those around Him. Still the old objection remains. All this is long ago. However wonderful it may all be, what properly religious data are there in it for us to-day? The data of religion are essentially present and living within the soul. All that has been said about Jesus is historical; that does not make it religious. This fact of Christ is a fact of history; it has

[1] Quoted in Hazlitt's essay on 'Persons one would wish to have seen.'

still to be shown how—as in the opening lecture was insisted—it contains the data of personal and spiritual religion.

The answer to this is still to 'think of' Jesus, to pursue to their issues these historical impressions. We shall find that to consider the fact of Christ has issues and that these are religious issues. We discover on the cold page of history this stainless one; and in a very wonderful and arresting way do thereupon our consciences discover, as never before, what kind of persons morally we are. We read an historic evangel—a proclamation made long ago by Jesus to all in moral need to listen to Him and to come to Him—and, as we read it, we growingly feel that this demands a decision on our part. All this is really religion, yet it is out of this fact of Christ that it has directly risen. Let us try to understand how we find our thoughts of Jesus thus turning into moral and religious channels.

What we find is this. We find that this fact of Christ, at all candidly considered in the conscience and the will, raises great moral issues within us. It is not merely that something in the example of Jesus or in His teaching has suggested a duty or made evident a defect. It is far more than that. It is that the problem of our whole moral life and character has been raised. The fact of Christ is not just a fact of history; it has become also a fact of conscience. It has arrested and arraigned our moral being; it has interrogated it; it has asserted itself as an authoritative reviewer of our life in the very fastnesses of our thoughts, our affections, and our will. It does so with a strange inevitableness and with a remarkable right to do it. The more we candidly keep our hearts and minds and consciences open to the impression that even an historical appreciation of the fact of Christ makes upon them, the more does that impression turn to moral issues within us. We had thought intellectually to examine Him; we find He is spirtually examining us. The *rôles* are reversed between us. Not that historical and intellectual questions on our part about Jesus end, but far more serious and pressing and immediate are these moral questions about ourselves that have arisen out of them. All this is found true by many and many an one who simply reads the Gospels. It is a very singular phenomenon. We study Aristotle and are intellectually edified thereby; we study Jesus and are, in the profoundest way, spiritually disturbed. The question—apparently so innocently historical and morally non-committal—of 'What think ye of Christ?' passes into the most morally practical and personal of questions: 'What shall I then do with Him?' And this presses for an answer.

For it comes to this. It comes to it that we are driven to do what it is a strange thing to do towards a figure of history. We are constrained to take up some inward moral attitude of heart and will in relation to this Jesus! or, to be more precise, we find we actually are doing so. We cannot escape it. A man may study Jesus with intellectual impartiality; he cannot do it with moral neutrality. If the words, the character, the person of Jesus at all awaken within us such issues as these, we cannot go on, nor can we even leave off, as if they never had been raised. Such questions, once asked, do have their answer; to try to ignore them is an an-

WHAT IS THE FACT? 53

swer as real as any other. And thus it is that, as I say, we are compelled to take up some attitude towards this fact of Christ. Whether we are going to have it that the inspiration and authority associated with Jesus are to be welcomed and cherished and obeyed, or whether we are going to evade them and resist them— this alternative becomes an inevitable question for us. Disguise it as we will to ourselves, we know we *are* answering it. What the answer is becomes the serious issue for our moral state and moral future. Indeed, here the great matter of our choice of a side in the perennial opposition between the good and the evil comes to a head. Ah! here is the war we spoke of. Here are no longer, merely, the 'confused alarms' of 'ignorant armies.' Here is the great conflict, near, real, personal; and we must declare our colors. To this has our unevasive contact with Jesus brought us. We began it in the calm of the study; we are called out to the field of moral decision, where, with some of us at least, are forces that will not yield without desperate struggle. We opened with the question of Jesus: now the question is

54   THE FACT OF CHRIST

about ourselves. And its answer depends on, or rather is, the attitude we take towards Him.

This may seem vague; this "attitude"—what is it? The most practical thing in the world. If we put aside the stereotyped terms of religious usage—not necessarily as false but as easily lending themselves to unreality—and face a few obvious facts of life, then the matter becomes not only clear but even rather clearer than at times we care that it should be. The alternative directions in life—in thought and in act—that lead, the one towards, the other away from, the inspiration and influence of Jesus, are not obscure. We know when we are honestly pressing towards Him and when we are keeping Him out of sight. In every man's life there are, both in little things and great, these alternative paths, and, at every serious moral choice, they diverge plainly before us. A man, seeing that the fact of Christ is becoming within him a fact of conscience with grave moral issues, may deliberately refuse to let it lead him further, and may, when any matter upon which it bears comes before him, take the path that does *not* lead to where the voice of Jesus would be more clear or His influence more authoritative. If so, it is no wonder that the primary fact of Christianity remains to him a merely historical externality, and that he does not find in it the data of religion. But a man may take the other course. There is much in the words of Jesus that calls him to this, and much in his own heart to admonish him to it. He may choose to follow the other way with strenuousness and simplicity, and if he does so,—and does so sincerely and with no *arrière-pensée* of adhering to evil things—then this fact of Christ becomes for him really a fact for religion. Christianity takes from it a meaning and a shape. The Jesus that was first the Jesus of history and criticism, and then the Jesus of conscience and of moral inspiration and decision, becomes now the Jesus of an inward experience of spiritual promise and wellbeing. The name of Jesus becomes in a remarkable way identical with the man's best self and his true life. Jesus is the man's true life, who with a hesitating astonishment finds himself putting a real, even if a small and variable, meaning into words he had always regarded as mere hyperbole—'I live yet not I, but Christ liveth in me.'

Now this—which I only indicate here and which we shall have occasion to pursue further and more carefully later—is religion. It is living, spiritual truths. It is not dead history. But it sprang out of history. It sprang out of the historical fact of Christ. It is all traceable back not to abstract ideas and principles but to that real phenomenon. 'Thinking of' Him has given us not only historical opinions but also the data of a faith. This fact, which begins in history, develops in the conscience and ends in religious experience, is indeed a fact on which religion can be built, and we find the ancient site of Christianity is still available for religion to-day.

This, then, is the fact of Christ—a fact of history, of conscience, and of spiritual experience. What we have to be careful about in stating the fact of Christ is that we state it completely. We do not state completely what Jesus is if we confine ourselves to an account of what He said and did and was in Palestine nineteen hundred years ago. Jesus is more

WHAT IS THE FACT?

than that. He is more than a fact of ancient history. He is also an ever-living fact of present or personal experience. You really do not do justice to the fact of Christ unless you thus treat it is, first indeed, an historical phenomenon, but also a phenomenon re-emerging and asserting itself in an unique way as a fact of consciousness—an inward arraignment, call, promise, renewal. You have not said what, as a matter of fact, He is unless you recognize both these elements. Neither is complete without the other. 'A perverted picture,' says a modern writer, 'is always the result when we take account of either the spiritual or the historical Christ to the exclusion of the other.'[1]

If, then, we are to build our Christianity upon the fact of Christ, it must not be upon a 'perverted picture,' upon a one-sided presentation of what the fact is. The fact is a dual fact. It is upon Christ as a fact alike of history and of experience that Christianity is based. We must hold to both of these aspects. If we con-

[1] Jess, *Uber den Christl. Glauben Vorträge*, p. 68 (quoted in Dr. Somerville's *St. Paul's Conception of Christ*).

fine ourselves merely to 'the Christ of history' in the sense of discussing a long dead teacher and his teaching, or if, on the other hand, we consider only 'the Christ of experience' without reference to what historically Jesus was, we shall fail to build on the wide and sure foundation. The foundation of Christianity is Christ. There are not two Christs on one or other of which we may build. There is but one Christ. But He is found alike in outward history and in inward experience. And our Christianity must be built upon the complete fact of Christ. 'The Christian religion,' as Professor Denney says, 'depends not only upon what He was, but upon what He is.'[1]—depends, in other words, upon a Christ who is a fact alike of history and of experience.

Our inquiry seems thus to be opening up as we proceed. We saw to begin with—very briefly, for it is a point which has often been established—that the original Christianity was based, not on theological or ethical ideas, but on the fact of the person of Jesus Himself. When we went on, as we have just been doing,

[1] *Studies in Theology*, p. 24.

to inquire if our Christianity could be built on this same site, we have found that it can, for this fact, while an historical event of nineteen hundred years ago, is also a fact of conscience and of moral life and experience in us to-day, and can thus be to us a source of present living truth, that is, a source of religion. We have thus not only found the authentic site; we find also that we can build upon it. With this building we must now proceed. That is to say, we now go on to examine and arrange and explicate what, for religion, is in this fact; in other words, we inquire into the meaning of the fact of Christ.

In beginning this, there is one thing which we must make very clear to ourselves. The whole success of our inquiry depends on our recognition of it.

It has been insisted upon that we must state and examine the complete fact of Christ. That complete fact is one not only of outward history, but also of inward experience. It is, therefore, obvious that there is needed for an inquiry into the meaning of such a fact more than simply the rational intelligence. That will discuss one aspect of it—the historical; and in its discussion of that, all the powers of the intelligence, aided by all the resources of scholarship, are welcome. But what is thus studied is not the whole fact of Christ, not the complete data of Christianity. That fact is also a fact of conscience; these data include a moral arraignment and choice and promise and experience. All this must be received as candidly as the other. If the fact of Christ, in one aspect of it, calls, like every other historical question, for the banishment of intellectual prejudice, in another aspect of it, the same fact calls for an honest conscience and an honest will. From the very nature of the case, from the dual character of the fact to be examined, you must, if you would really and thoroughly study Christianity, study it, with a critical intelligence indeed, for Jesus is a fact of history, but also with more than a critical intelligence—with a conscience and will that are open to moral impression and direction, for He is also a fact of inward moral experience. If you would know what Christianity is you must be open and honest in both directions. If your investigation of the fact of Christ discloses some historical point, you must have a candid mind for that. So much every one will admit. But if your investigation brings you face to face—as it will do, for this is a fact of conscience as well as of history—with some moral choice and moral call, then, not less, you must have a candid will to receive that. This is apparent from the very nature of the subject that is investigated, from its dual nature as alike outward and inward. Let us make this matter clear to ourselves. Let us distinctly perceive that we shall never understand what Christianity is if we have a morally evasive or dishonest will. Let us perceive there is a reason for this—namely, because the fact of Christ, in which are the data of Christianity, is a fact of conscience as well as of history. We must then meet that fact with moral as well as mental candor, with not only a mind open to historical facts but also a will honest with moral issues. Otherwise is it not obvious that our whole discussion is doomed from the outset? In insisting on this, we are still only following the method of the great Master of

Religion, for it was particularly to the man 'that willeth to do His will,' even more than to the man of intellectual superiority or historical erudition, that Jesus promised that he 'shall know of the doctrine.'

III

THE FIRST MEANING OF THE FACT

Τούτων ἤδη προδιηνυσμένων, ἑπόμενον ἂν εἴη τὸν παιδαγωγὸν ἡμῶν Ἰησοῦν τὸν βίον ἡμῖν τὸν ἀληθινὸν ὑποτυπώσασθαι, καὶ τὸν ἐν Χριστῷ παιδαγωγῆσαι ἄνθρωπον.
CLEMENT OF ALEXANDRIA.

III

THE FIRST MEANING OF THE FACT

THE meaning of Christ is a large word. Such a pivotal fact—pivotal in the realms alike of universal history and of individual experience—is surely not, as Aristotle would say, a mere episode in a badly composed play. If human history have a meaning, and if spiritual experience have a meaning, then the fact of Christ has a meaning. So great a fact must indeed have great meanings, and it should not surprise us if, in the end, we find these stretching out beyond what we are able fully to explain or even to express.

But however the question of the meaning of the fact of Christ may develop, there is no difficulty about making a beginning in the answering of it. Christ has at least some meanings that are immediate and plain and simple. I think I shall express the mind of perhaps most of us if I say that the first of these is a meaning for moral life and character.[1]

This has indeed already appeared in the mere statement of the fact of Christ. Historically we have found Him to be an ideal, supreme and stainless; in the inner realm of conscience we find Him to be a moral authority, personal and pressing. No man can really open his mind and conscience to the fact of Christ without feeling that he ought to be a better man, and that, if he and Christ are to continue near each other, he must be a better man. His faults are named to him and his duties as never before. Whatever else the fact of Christ means, it means this; and a man well knows that any attempt to lose sight of this meaning by a professed earnestness about any other is a palpable evasion. Christ indubitably means this much—that you revise your life and conduct and character by a new standard, that

[1] The way in which the fact of Christ approaches the mind and becomes meaningful of course varies. The meanings here discussed last are often the first and immediate. But some order or other must be chosen, and that I have adopted seems, on general grounds, natural and logical, and is intelligible even to those whose personal experience may not have followed it.

THE FIRST MEANING 67

you set before yourself new ideas of what you will be and do, and that you set out to realize these. Where this is not felt, it were far better for a man to admit that he is not facing and will not face the fact of Christ. The example of Jesus in history and the authority of Jesus in experience alike mean this. And thus the question of our character at once arises in Christianity as a part of the meaning of Christ. Whatever else it does, Christianity proposes to us a new character, and it also—for without this the other would be futile—declares the way of its achievement. Both of these things we must examine a little.

One may observe, before going on to these points, how notable and also how effective is this element in the religion of Jesus. That a religion should concern itself with character is to us a matter of course; but this was far from being the case in the great world into which the young Christian gospel made its way. In the civilization of the Roman empire—a civilization, in some respects, more elaborate than ours—religion was something absolutely apart from morality. The priests and augurs of ancient Greece and Rome never for one moment regarded it as any part of their duty to exhort or help men to a purer life. Alike public life and private were steeped in a heartlessness of cruelty and an abandonment of vice such as we can hardly realize; but pagan religion made no protest, for, on the contrary, its mysteries often screened and its ministers sanctioned the grossest iniquities. It is this entire divorce between religion and morality in the ancient world which supplies the explanation, as Mr. Lecky has pointed out,[1] of the apparently strange circumstance that the classical philosophic moralists pay so little attention to the appearance of Christianity. One would suppose that that religion, as a mere system of ethics, apart from any theological beliefs would have commanded the notice of all serious men. But—so we can imagine the philosophers who were in earnest about moral things, saying—is this not a religion? and what has a religion to do with the matter of moral life? Thus argued, and most naturally, such men as Plutarch, or Seneca, or

[1] *History of European Morals*, i. 336 *et sqq.*

Epictetus, or Marcus Aurelius, and thus before the eyes of these great moralists emerged what was to be the supreme moral phenomenon of history, and they gave it hardly a glance. How were they to know that this religion was to belie all their natural anticipation of the scope and purpose of religion, was going to unite itself so emphatically and essentially with morals, and was going to mean, almost before anything else, a new moral character for men. If such thoughts had been even for a moment conceivable, surely a Seneca would have had a word about that Christianity with some of the tenets of which his own writings supply so interesting a parallel,[1] and surely history might have been spared what has justly been called one of its 'most tragical facts,'[2] that a Marcus Aurelius should have persecuted the followers of Jesus Christ.

But, not to dwell on this, what is the character which Christianity has brought into the world?

[1] *Vide* Lightfoot's Dissertation on Seneca and St. Paul in his Commentary on *Philippians*.
[2] J. S. Mill's *Essay on Liberty*, ii.

I. THE CHRISTIAN CHARACTER

The norm of the Christian character is of course the character of Jesus Himself. He is its 'living law,'[1] as an early apologist terms it. We must, therefore, in the first place, form some definite impression of what were the distinctive features of the character of Jesus. I say distinctive, for, of course, there were in Him many qualities—such as courage or truth or fidelity—which are not peculiarly Christian, and these we do not need to dwell on here. Our aim at present is not to discuss all the aspects of the character that Jesus exhibited on earth, but to recognize those that are distinctively and specially what we call Christian. It is these we wish to observe.

There were, I think, four such elements in the character of Jesus.

The first of these were purity or holiness. I call this distinctive because Jesus was not only, as has been said, a perfectly unstained man, but the only man to whom such a word as purity or holiness can be applied without any reserva-

[1] Lactantius, *Divin. Instit.* iv. 25.

tion whatever. Among the moral teachers and heroes of the extra-Christian world are many who admired and practiced virtue to an eminent degree; but there is not one of whom we should say that to him the very thought of impurity of any kind was abhorrent and with whom the imagination shrinks from associating the bare suggestion of evil. It is Jesus who has introduced into virtue a passion before which vice is not condemned but consumed as by fire. It is He who has charged the ethical nature with an intolerable radiance and raised it to a white heat. And thus what we call purity—the virtue that is intense and vivid and sensitive to the very suggestion of sin—has, through Him, entered into the moral ideal of human character. He has made virtue a wholly new thing—an inward, refining passion in the soul. He has taught His people to pray: 'O God, make clean our hearts within us.' Clean, transparent, pellucid as a hillside spring in which all that is turbid and foul has sunk, and which reflects in all its depths only the sweet, glad light of heaven! Who has suggested to the sin-befouled soul of man such a thought of virtue as this? Who has shown the way to its realization? He has who out of His own experience said, 'Blessed are the pure in heart for they shall see God.'

The second distinctive feature in the character of Jesus was love. This, too, in its true and Christian sense He created. The apprehension of what love really is and of the place it should have in human life came into the world with Jesus and had never been understood before. This is not to say that human nature, apart from Jesus, had no idea of what love is; but He so enlarged, so intensified, and so exalted that idea as to produce a practically new creation. He enlarged it. He made it a universal thing. It had been at best a limited thing, and even so elevated a teacher as Plato applauded an 'unadulterated hate'[1] of a foreigner. The very name for foreigner was to the Greek the same as that for barbarian, to the Roman the same as that for enemy. If the ancients knew love at all, they did not know its universal realm. Jesus has showed us that love is of humanity; that had never been thought

[1] *Menaxenus*, 245.

of in the Porch or the Academy. And He not only thus enlarged the idea of love, but He also intensified it. If it be said that the Stoic philosophers, at least, approached the idea of universal brotherhood, be it admitted. Yet what a new thing to a Stoic was the love of His brother-men that was in Jesus. The former's view of the relation of man to man was, at best, a tepid, theoretical affair; even when a Stoic was humane—and he was far from always being that—he was studiously temperate and restrained in his humanity. The love of Jesus for men was an enthusiasm. It was a heart's love He gave them and its activities were pulsing with His heart's blood. In His love to men He yearned over them, and prayed for them, and labored for them, and, in the end, He died for them. This was indeed a new love, that amid the cold of the first Christmas came upon the world like the heat of a midsummer sun and its warmth has never died since out of the heart of man. And again, Jesus who made love universal and ardent, made it also the first and supreme law of life. There have been in history many noble deeds of self-sacrificing devotion. But He made love the law—the guiding principle of life and of all life. It was His life to love, and He had no other life than love. He was love. In all these ways, then, Jesus so renewed the idea of love—so enlarged it, intensified it, and exalted it—as really to create it. The world had never seen love after this sort. And if love after this sort—love that is towards all, that will do anything and that is recognized as life's first law—has a place in the ideal of human character, that dates from Him, who, even literally,[1] has re-created the name of love in the world.

The third distinctive feature in the character of Jesus was forgiveness. This, of course, springs out of the last, and yet it must be mentioned by itself, for it is, while not the greatest, perhaps the most distinct innovation that Jesus made in morality. The general feeling on the

[1] The word 'love,' to us one of the most elevated in the language, had in ancient classical use a very different reputation, and even in the fourth century, Jerome, writing the Vulgate (in Latin) could not use the ordinary word *amor* to express the Christian grace of love, and had recourse to the unusual *caritas*. Hence the use of the word 'charity' in our A. V.

THE FIRST MEANING 75

subject in the pre-Christian world is well exhibited in the famous inscription which Plutarch tells us was written on the monument to Sulla in the Campus Martius at Rome: 'No friend ever did me so much good or enemy so much harm but I repaid him with interest.' Forgiveness was a thing not unknown to the ancient mind as an idea, but it was not really expected of any one in practice. Jesus made it operative. He treasured no resentments, kept no wrongs green, harbored no implacability, had never a moment's thought of revenge; and, not this only, but He acted daily in the spirit of that prayer on the Cross, which, more than anything, must have made the Roman centurion wonder and watch till he worshipped: 'Father, forgive them, for they know not what they do.' What an innovation was here! This law of forgiveness 'has produced,' says the author of *Ecce Homo,* 'so much impression upon mankind that it is commonly regarded as the whole or at least the fundamental part of the Christian moral system,' and 'when a Christian spirit is spoken of it may be remarked that a forgiving spirit is usually meant.'[1]

There is, however, yet a fourth feature in the moral character of Jesus which was original and distinctive as much as any other, and that was humility. That this is peculiarly Christian hardly needs to be said. In the pagan world, anything approaching to it was despised, and the very virtues of the best ethical schools were founded on a self-pride. The humility of Jesus may appear to be a feature of hardly such importance that it should be ranked with the others that have been mentioned, but to think this is to fail to appreciate what a place it had in His life. Of course humility is not conspicuous; just because it is humility it is always the flower

> 'Half-hidden from the eye.'

And in this, humility is always to be distinguished from self-humilation, with which mediæval religion tended to identify it, and which may be, and often is, obvious and ostentatious. Humility must be looked for if we

[1] *Ecce Homo,* ch. xxii, from which one or two thoughts in this paragraph are taken.

would discover it, like eidelweiss upon the Alps. But when we find it in perfection, as we do in Jesus, how beautiful it is! It was not only that He was utterly free from vulgar vanity and restless self-seeking, that he never even listened for applause nor looked towards the place of the popular hero. It was far more than that. If ever there was a master among men it was He; yet He was among them as one that serveth. If ever there was a teacher of genius it was He; yet He counted an afternoon not wasted that was spent with the Samaritan woman, nor a life lost that was lived, for the most part, with the poor, the unlearned, the uninteresting—as men often judge—of the land. He who was the supreme person in history is best described as the friend of publicans and sinners. This was the humility of Jesus. It is a revelation of the true greatness. There is at times something impressive and fascinating about the lordly egotism of a Cæsar or a Napoleon—men who seem almost of right to regard themselves as of another than the common clay, and the rest of men as made but to swell the train of their triumph. Yet we see in Jesus, who incomparably more than these world-conquerors was one above His fellows, and who, moreover, knew His power over them—'Ye call Me,' He said, 'Master and Lord, and ye say well, for so I am'—something that impresses us far more than a proud 'bestriding of the narrow world like a colossus,' and which stirs us to a deeper reverence than we ever give to them. Jesus had power, but He baptized His power with the spirit of humble service. He was a world-lord, but He was the lowly among His inferiors. He was the Master, yet He ministered. Thus has He taught us a new and the true grandeur of life. It was one of the supreme moral triumphs of His career, and, with forgiveness, its most original feature. And there is in men to-day perhaps no feature which more distinctly tells that a new influence has come to operate on human character than a spirit that has learned of Him who was 'meek and lowly of heart,' and that 'has let this mind be in it' which was also in the humble spirit of Jesus; for there is so much in the natural man that dislikes and disputes this that it is a peculiar sign of the

THE FIRST MEANING

character which is Christian. 'Wellnigh the whole substance of the Christian discipline,' says Augustine, ' is humility.' [1]

Purity, love, forgiveness, humility—these are four distinctive features of the character of Jesus. No one can have to do with the fact of Christ—either historically in the record of His life and teaching, or inwardly in the moral issues which He raises—without having these things set before him. Whatever else Christianity has in it, surely and urgently to be a Christian means to be pure, to be loving, to be forgiving, and to be humble. This moral meaning of Jesus for life and character we cannot deny and cannot honestly evade.

But if we cannot deny it and cannot honestly evade it, how shall we really achieve it? It is easy to speak of purity, but how shall I, with any sincerity, cleanse my heart? It is pleasant to write of love, but how almost irresistibly difficult to be wholly unselfish? It is a fine thing to laud forgiveness, but, when I am hurt and wronged, it is not in human nature easily to forget it. It is not hard to affect to be hum-

[1] *Ser. de Pœnit*, i. 4.

ble, but it is very hard to be humble. A very slight practical observation and experiment in these things will soon discover to us that they do not evolve themselves within us, and that they are ideals we like to praise but are unready too strictly to practice. We lie on the plains of life and look and talk of the heights of purity and love and forgiveness and humility; but when it comes to climbing them, how human nature is laggard, is impotent, is positively unwilling and opposed to it! No man who knows himself will deny that.

And yet these heights have by many been scaled. No one can survey the Christian centuries without admitting that Jesus has not only meant this kind of character, but, despite this practical opposition to it in human nature, has, to a very marked degree, meant it effectively. Men have learned of Jesus not only what this character is, but that it may be theirs. The Christian character—the character that is pure, loving, forgiving, humble—has, to an undeniable extent, been achieved in many lives. Most of us, I imagine, have seen it—seen it perhaps in lives that have passed from our sight, leaving us as their sacred legacy, an impression of the reality and beauty of what is Christian that nothing can efface. The character that is Christian is not a natural evolution, but it is a fact.

It is then a fact that calls for some explanation. What has made men pure, loving, forgiving, humble? What will make *me* all this? The ideal of the Christian character is not enough; where and what is the moral dynamic that will realize it in human nature? Can we find in the fact of Christ this, too?

II. THE MORAL MOTIVE-POWER

The loved late Henry Drummond—whose own character was a singularly clear example of those who, as I have just been saying, show to us that the Christian character can be achieved in human nature—begins his little brochure entitled *The Changed Life* by quoting the following well-known words of Huxley: ' I protest that if some great power would agree to make me always think what is true and do what is right on condition of being turned into a sort of clock and wound up every morning,

I should instantly close with the offer,'[1] and then he proceeds: 'I propose to make that offer now: in all seriousness, without being "turned into a sort of clock," the end can be attained.'[2] It is a bold reply. Is there anything which the fact of Christ means which can make it good?

In answering this question the things to be carefully watched and avoided are unreality and exaggeration. When one is speaking of historical facts, it is easy to detect these faults, but when one is speaking of such a topic as inward moral power, they are faults into which it is very easy to fall. There is a conscience in all teaching, especially about experimental things; and I do not know any way in which that conscience is more prostituted than when, on this very topic, a man speaks loosely, and indulges in assertions that have not facts behind them.

The first question for us to ask is plainly this: What kind of a motive-power is it that expresses itself in what we call a character? To this question, answers seem apparent and

[1] 'Essay on Descartes' *(Selected Essays,* p. 139).
[2] *Addresses,* p. 179. ('The Changed Life,' init.)

simple. We may say it is our choice or our will; or we may say that it is the force of an inspiring example or a strong command. Such answers may be sufficient when we are considering character on its ordinary levels, but they are not sufficient when the springs of character in its loftiest or deepest levels are sought. They are not then sufficient when we ask the motive-power of the Christian character. They are not a sufficient motive-power to produce purity, love, forgiveness, humility. Choice and will are not, for we must often admit with the Apostle that 'the good which I would, I do not, and the evil which I would not that I do'; example is not, for we must admit with the Roman poet,

'Video meliora proboque, deteriora sequor';[1]

while a bare command to such moral excellences as those of the Christian ideal is obviously non-effective. The motive-power we seek must be something more than any of these.

What more is it? If not merely choice or

[1] Ovid, *Met.* iii. 19 ('I see and approve the better; I follow the worse').

will or an example or a command suffices to achieve character in its highest and deepest forms, therefore not in the Christian form, what does? Well, what really makes your character is the kind of *spirit* that is in you. It is of course difficult to define this, and perhaps I shall make my meaning most clear by an example. Take the example of patriotism. What makes the patriotic character? Not just the choice of it as a fine and noble ideal; not just the assiduous imitation of the habits and deeds of a Nelson or a Washington; not just the command of a government. Something, including, perhaps, all these, but also deeper and subtler. There must be stirred up what we call the patriotic spirit. Create that in men and cherish it, and the patriotic character is already there and will express itself in life spontaneously and inevitably. So is it with any other high or deep form of character. It is not manufactured, it is not a studied process; it is 'born of the spirit,' and being so born can do almost anything that that spirit requires.

Now if this is to be said of a type of character such as the patriotic, it is to be said with tenfold emphasis of such a type as the Christian. The patriotic spirit is indeed a fine and admirable thing, but yet not a thing so lofty as to be unattainable by various human means. But the spirit, the very spirit, of purity, of love, of forgiveness, of humility—how that is too high for us! The externalities of these are hardly reached by us, and who shall bring down their very inspiration? If the white flowers of the Christian moral ideal grow almost too far up the mountain for our hands and feet to get to them, how hopelessly inaccessible is the sun in whose streaming light the flowers have grown! If we do not even attain to the acts of Christian character, how shall we attain to the spirit of it? And yet, if what has been said in the foregoing paragraph be true, the only motive-power that will achieve that character is the creating and cherishing in us of *the spirit of Jesus*. We seem to have made for ourselves an *impasse*.

Let us remember what was said about the importance, in discussing these things, of a conscientious regard to facts, and let us try to base our way out, not—as is so easily done—on moral rhetoric, but on certain recorded facts of history.

In the first place let us note that Jesus Himself regarded the imparting to men of a new spirit as the one thing that would make them right. 'Except a man be born again,' He said to one of His most interesting inquirers, 'he cannot see the kingdom of God,' and this He explained to mean a being re-born spiritually or 'of the spirit.' Jesus regarded this as axiomatic, and therefore His moral aim and mission on earth were not simply to teach morals, or even simply exemplify them, but— it is His own phrase—'baptize with the spirit.' And that He succeeded in this, His transformation of a John and a Peter, a Mary Magdalene and countless others shows. Most literally and obviously He put into them a new spirit,— His own spirit of purity, love, forgiveness, and humility—and thus made them new characters.

We can understand this so long as Jesus actually was living on earth. The spirit of a great personality enters into those who come into actual contact with him. A brave man inspires the spirit of bravery in others by his

THE FIRST MEANING 87

presence; a pure soul purifies us when we are with him. And when one thinks of what a marvellous personality that of Jesus was, one can believe that those who met Him, and heard His voice, and felt His glance, not only were impressed by His words, but were really changed in their whole nature, and yielded themselves to His spirit. If Napoleon could have this influence on his army, certainly Jesus could have it on His friends. But this has limits. This kind of influence on men's spirits demands one thing—that the author of it be himself present. It is essentially personal, and where the personal element is wanting, the spiritual inspiration fades. And therefore, obviously, when a great man dies, the influence of his personality passes. It remains for a while in the hearts of those who knew him, and it may remain for future ages as a great memory and example. But all this is but a phantom of the man's personal inspiration. He is no longer there. We must seek new inspirations.

It would thus appear that, while we can understand that Jesus, so long as He was living on this earth, was able literally to put a new spirit into the minds and hearts and wills of those He met (and therefore enable them to realize even the Christian character), all this was only while and only because He was personally alive and present with them; and when He passed from this earth, we should expect it to pass, too. It does not appear therefore that there is anything in all this to put a new spirit in us to-day, who have never seen His face nor heard His voice.

But it is here that we meet with by far the most remarkable phenomenon both of the New Testament and of all moral history.

In the utterances of Jesus recorded in the Gospel narratives—which are here regarded simply as historical records—we find a very singular point of view emerging on this subject. Jesus, as has been said, exerted a marvellous spiritual influence by His personality during His life; but, as that earthly life was drawing to its close, we do not find Him contemplating the withdrawal or diminution of that influence. The very contrary. He promised its persistence and even its augmentation. That

THE FIRST MEANING

very spirit with which He had baptized men, and which it only too inevitably seemed must pass with His earthly presence, is the very thing which, most impressively, He declared would be given more than ever. By this spirit, He clearly meant certainly nothing less than all that His present personality had been; and indeed His meaning He often simply expressed by saying that He—all that the personal contact with Himself had meant—would not pass. It is this note which is the most remarkable characteristic of the latter phases of the utterances of Jesus. There is nothing like it in the later teaching of any other man. He sums it up in His last recorded words: 'I am with you always, even unto the end of the world.' Consider these words. Imagine that they were the last words to us of some loved friend or some trusted leader. How infinitely sad and pathetic would they be! And why? Simply because they were not and could not be really, fully, literally true. They might have a certain amount of poetic truth. Something remains with us—a dear memory, a great example. Something remains, but, ah, not he!

Not the loved presence, not the potent personal inspiration: there remains not *he!* We will not say he is extinct, and that which was a soul is clay; but only too clearly, he is not here as once he was. And we are lonelier, and sadder, and poorer because he is not with us. If, therefore, I say, some loved friend of ours or leader left us saying, 'I am with you always,' how pathetic it would be. These were the last words of Jesus.

Let us turn now to the other writings of the New Testament—not, I repeat, as inspired authorities, but as records. What do we find? This pathetic sense of irreparable personal loss, the constant sigh that He were here to guide and strengthen and inspire, the sad refrain—'Now He is dead'? This is the note we should expect in the New Testament, a kind of 'In Memoriam' strain. But we find that every page is simply throbbing with the utter opposite. Every book is filled with the witness to it that the last words of Jesus are found fully, literally true. His great idea had been towards the end of His earthly life that all that spiritually He had been to men—all that

He was for men, above mere precept and example, in His personality—would continue a living spirit within them. The New Testament writers' chief thesis—I say it deliberately—is that this is so. The spirit of Jesus moving them, moulding them, transforming them as really, as directly, as powerfully, as personally as when He walked on earth and spoke to them —that is unquestionably the great feature of New Testament literature. There is nothing like it in any other literature in the world. All the writers are agreed about it. St. John finds that Jesus is not a fading ideal, but 'has given us of His spirit.' St. Peter, who knew Jesus so well in history, finds Him still present in inward life in His spirit 'which is in thee.' St. James, in almost parallel words, speaks of it 'dwelling in us.' St. Paul finds Jesus to be just as much a victorious moral dynamic against evil as ever His personal presence on earth was, and declares that 'the spirit of life in Jesus Christ has made us free from the law of sin.' I have given four quotations; but any one who reads the New Testament knows that the number can be made unlimited. I repeat that the most notable and unmistakable thing in the New Testament is this assertion that all that Jesus had been He still was found to be, that He was not a dead memory, but a living spirit. His last words were no pathetic fiction; He *was* with them, in them a spirit, a power, a presence, a personality as much as ever in the days of His flesh.

Now what does all this mean? It is an impressive witness—the combination of the distinct forecast of Jesus that it would be so and the unwavering assertion of the early Christian writers that it had proved to be so. Does it all mean no more than that a great and good man's influence is a powerful legacy to the moral force of the world, or that the New Testament writers, when they speak of 'Christ living in them' by His spirit, mean only that His ideas profoundly influenced them still? Those who say the former think by a platitude to account for what is the most remarkable phenomenon in history—the triumphant rise of the Christian church immediately after the death of its Founder; those who say the latter make the New Testament the most inflated and exaggerated religious book in the world and therefore one of the worst, for what is worse than a spirituality that is not sane and a religiousness that has no conscience about facts? And yet what does it mean to us—the spirit of Jesus still living about us and within us?

A previous lecture has been enough to show us that it is not all utterly meaningless. We found the fact of Christ to be more than a bare fact of ancient history; we found it to be also an inward authority and appeal and persuasion. And what is this but at least the beginning of finding that Jesus is spirit and life within us? Alike the man who resists it and the man who yields to it and obeys it confess this.

There is such a thing as resisting the appeal and authority and influence of Jesus. Have not many of us—if we really ask ourselves—done this distinctly, persistently, emphatically? Have we not at times said a 'No' to something in His words or example with a loudness that almost startled ourselves? But why this expenditure of energy? Why call up our resolution to take arms against a precept or an example of nineteen hundred years ago? We do not so resist Aristotle even when he speaks to us of ethical things; we can decline to obey him without that expenditure. But when we really let Jesus speak to us by His words and examples, if we are going not to obey, we must and do definitely and often determinedly say ' No.' Again, I ask, why this expenditure of energy? Let us learn from the active reality of our resistance the active reality of what we are resisting. It is not simply an old ethical precept nor a far ethical example. It is something more active, more living. It is 'spirit and life.' It is Jesus appealing to us to-day with just the same spiritual, personal presence with which, as we can well understand, He did to the rich young ruler or the woman of Samaria. There are times when our very refusal of something in Christianity, by its very heat, discloses itself to be a refusal of far more than an idea or precept, like the ideas or precepts of, say, Epictetus. A spirit touched and moved and almost persuaded us in it all; therefore was our 'No' so peculiarly distinct a thing. It is an unwilling witness that Jesus is not a dead tradition of precept or example,

THE FIRST MEANING

but is still all that living spiritual personality can be.

If this be forced upon us by our refusals of Him, how shall we say that it is clear to us by our yieldings to Him? Let us avoid all vagueness and unreality. Let us start from what is plain and practical. When Jesus was speaking of this spiritual realization of Himself He reached to lofty mystical heights, but He connected it with things quite near. In particular He connected it with His words—that is, alike His commands and promises. Let a man really face these, and meditate on them, and apply them to his life, and realize their meaning. What then? He finds he is doing far more than merely reading 'words, words, words.' He is opening unseen forces upon his mind and conscience and heart and will—forces that enlighten and quicken and purify and enable him in a way that is a surprise to himself. A day thus lived is lived in a new spirit—in the spirit of Jesus. And have we created that in ourselves? Have mere ethical precepts, however elevated, done it? Surely the apostle's account of it is the only just one. 'We are changed . . . by the Spirit *which is the Lord.*' Only Jesus Himself, only His living personality, gives us the spirit of Jesus. The most remarkable phenomenon of spiritual literature finds its echo in the fact of our moral history, and what account of it can we give but this—that whereas the personalities, with all contained therein, of all other moral and spiritual leaders must pass away with the passing of their earthly career, ' there is one grand exception to this rule?'[1] The spirit—as something more than example and precept—which Jesus, when on earth was able, as we can understand, to inspire into the spirits of those He met, He still gives to us to-day. In short, *He is* ' with us.' His personal presence—with all the inspiration that is in personal presence—has changed its form; it is no longer in the flesh. But it abides in essence and in reality. It is spirit, and

' Spirit with spirit can meet.'[2]

It can—I should rather say He can, for spirit is essentially a man's personality—inform our

[1] Principal Caird's *Fundamental Ideas of Christianity,* ii. 237.   [2] Tennyson's *Higher Pantheism.*

spirits, and if our spirits are informed by the spirit of Jesus, then our lives will assuredly exhibit the otherwise unattainable ideal of the Christian character. 'The Lord'—the Lawgiver of the new ideal morality—' is the Spirit'—the inspiration of it.

This, then, is the meaning of the fact of Christ for character—its twofold meaning. Jesus is at once its ideal and the power that inspires men to its achievement. This meaning that Jesus has in the realm of character is without even an approach to a parallel in the whole ethical world. The world's masters of morals have simply trifled with the question of character in comparison with Jesus. What as a real solution of the problem of human character—what it is for man to be good, and how man actually is to be made good—are the discussions of Aristotle, the aphorisms of Bacon, even the virtues of Socrates or the example of Gautama, in comparison with what Jesus has done first by His example and teaching, and then, even more wonderfully, by His enduring personal spiritual presence and power giving to men that very spirit by which alone a character can be realized? In this domain His name holds the field.

And is not this a great thing for each one of us personally, as well as a great thing for the world at large? In our truest moments we know that, after all, *the* question of our lives is the question of our character. Our most profound and significant success or failure is not in the secondary issues on which the world judges us, but is there. Indeed, it looks as if this strange life of ours were made only for character. Not only the world of conscience within suggests this, but also the world of circumstance without. For all other purposes—the making of fortune, the enjoyment of pleasure, the securing of worldly wealth or position or fame—this is a life ill-adapted. The flux of things, the uncertainties of fate, the varied unforeseen combinations of circumstances adverse to or destructive of health or wealth or happiness—all these make life a place obviously not formed primarily for these ends, the attempt to gain which is so easily and often thwarted, and which, even when gained, are held on so uncertain a tenure. This is really not the world for worldliness. But observe that all these conditions—this flux, this risk, this uncertainty—are the very conditions that help to form character. They make just the discipline by which a man may become tender and spiritual, patient and humble, unselfish and loving. The circumstances of life may defeat all other ends, but they cannot defeat, and they even must contribute towards, this end. And so I say that it looks as if life were made for character. And if this be so, then surely life can never be properly or prosperously lived without Him who is the only person who has dealt with the problem of human character fully and effectively. To this extent, therefore, and at least so far as this first meaning of the fact of Christ goes, should not every one of us seek to be a Christian?

IV

THE FURTHER MEANING OF THE FACT

'Du den wir suchen auf so finstern Wegen
Mit forschenden Gedanken nicht erfassen,
Du hast dein heilig Dunkel einst erlassen
Und tratest sichtbar deinem Volk entgegen.'
—UHLAND.

IV

THE FURTHER MEANING OF THE FACT

ABOUT the meaning of the fact of Christ which we have just discussed one thing is plain—that it is not the full meaning of that fact. It clearly raises questions that call for further investigation. If it be the first meaning of the fact it is only the first. This meaning must itself have a meaning. We have already said about Jesus more—incomparably more—than can be said of any other man, but just because we have said so much we must say more still. With no mental satisfaction can we halt at the present stage. To say that Jesus Himself exhibited an absolutely stainless and ideal character, and that moreover, He is able, though His form left this earth centuries ago, still to be an inspiration of the most personal kind in men's hearts, by which they, too, are, at least to some degree, enabled to realize that otherwise impossible ideal—to say all this and then lay down the pen is utterly inconclusive. If it be ethically and spiritually impossible to say less, then it is intellectually incumbent to say more. The finding of this first meaning of the fact of Christ is the setting before us of new questions that need a further answer.

The questions thus raised are of the following kind. Is a phenomenon in history and experience, such as has been described, not one of quite peculiar and commanding significance for our philosophy of life and nature? Can it be accounted for along with, and in the same way as, other phenomena? May we not, and must we not, 'amid the darkness of the world,' accept it 'as throwing a vivid and particular light on the nature of the force that is guiding the destinies of man and of the soul?'[1] May we not through it find some foundation for a faith—for some real assurance concerning a God such as our spirits seek and often seek in vain?

Ever since Jesus was in this world, men have

[1] Mrs. Humphry Ward in the *Times*, September 5, 1899.

never been able to rid themselves of the feeling that in Him, if at all, is the quest of faith most likely to find its answer. The fact of this is indisputable and it is of extraordinary significance. His very first associates felt it when their spokesman said: 'Lord, to whom shall we go? Thou hast the words of eternal life.' His very last and latest students feel it, and the authoress of *Robert Elsmere* writes in the year of grace 1899 to the *Times* (in the earnest and interesting letter quoted above) that the school she represents still 'say as Peter said of old,' not indeed from Peter's standpoint, but with Peter's persuasion that there is the light to be sought. Think of that far fisherman in Galilee and of this writer of to-day in England, and of the inconceivable difference of their whole intellectual atmosphere and surrounding and point of view; and yet both, in the soul's search for God, unable to turn away from that figure. Think of the unceasing and innumerable inquirers who, during the intervening centuries, have confessed the same. And is not already a *prima facie* case made out that in the fact of

Christ is something of entirely unique significance for the great problem of faith?

There is thus ample reason, alike from the meaning we have already found in the fact of Christ, and from the feeling of earnest minds in all the Christian ages towards that fact, to go on to ask the questions that have been indicated. In doing so let us not think that we are leaving the simple data of Christianity and are plunging into the dogmas of theology. It is still the fact of Christ we are investigating, still that living fact of history and experience; it is not theological theory. In passing, then, from questions of character to questions of faith, our inquiry need not, to use Goethe's metaphor, assume the 'greyness' of 'all theory,' but should preserve the glow and verdure of life.[1]

1. The Foundation of Faith

The quest of faith is not simply an intellectual exercise in dialectic as to whether there be a God—a first principle of which all things are the manifestation and the result. It is far

---

[1] 'Grau, theurer freund, is alle Theorie,
Und grün des Lebens goldner baum.'—FAUST.

more than that. It is essentially a personal quest, undertaken not by the speculative side of man's nature, but by the whole of his nature, and therefore what it seeks is not a mere category of thought, but what will meet and satisfy personal needs. Whether or not this be a hopeless quest, certainly not less than this is what the human spirit—something much more profound, complex, and passionate than a merely intellectually speculative spirit—has ever sought and ever will seek. It never found simpler, yet truer and more pathetic utterance than in the old words of the exiled Hebrew psalmist: 'My soul is athirst for God, even the living God.'

There is a tendency in certain philosophical quarters to regard a prayer such as this almost with contempt. We are sometimes exhorted that we should be above this fond yearning after a personal Friend and Father of our spirits, and should be able to stand, sad a little, perhaps, but strong, in our philosophy; and that even such a desire as that for immortality is in reality a selfishness which it is the nobler part to renounce. There is not a little of this suggested to us in modern philosophy and literature. Goethe suggested it to us, and Hegel, George Eliot, and Matthew Arnold. I believe this to be an utterly false resignation, an entirely spurious heroism, 'which prides itself on being able to renounce what never *ought* to be renounced.'[1] Man never ought to renounce these yearnings after a personal God and a personal immortality, for in these are his true self and his true dignity. His true self is his personal individuality, and 'over-against its I, it seeks a Thou, and will rest satisfied with nothing less.'[2] It is not treating man as man to bid him be satisfied with less. It is an act of spiritual suicide which, with whatever philosophical glory it may disguise itself, is still dishonorable; 'such honor rooted in dishonor stands.' The true dignity of man is in these very personal needs which sometimes we would be too intellectually dignified to confess. These prayers may be in vain. We may seek the Father—the living, personal Father—of our

---

[1] Professor Seth's *Scottish Philosophy*, vi.
[2] Professor Orr's *Christian View of God and the World*, p. 135.

THE FURTHER MEANING 109

spirits and *not* find; we may knock at the gates of everlasting life and they may *not* be opened. But the seeking, the knocking—it is these by which man declares, not his littleness, but his greatness, not the smallness of selfishness but the infinity that is in and that is himself. That is indeed a poor honor which man pays himself in bidding himself attain to be satisfied to be but a part of finite nature.

Whether or not this search for the Father of our spirits will find its answer in the fact of Christ, it is clear that it is not satisfied by the facts of outward nature, of history, or of even the moral realm within. I shall speak of this only briefly. Nature tells us of great forces, impersonal and unconscious, indifferent to, and apparently ever antagonistic to, the hap and hopes of man. There is an aspect of Nature that is benign and beautiful, but there is also an aspect that is bloody and brutal; there is one view in which she seems full of marvellous thought for even the smallest thing, but in another view how little she seems to feel for even her noblest works, flinging them aside to perish in utter heartlessness. There is no answer here to faith; there are indeed but 'evil dreams.' Nature does not meet but only mocks our quest with her baffling and often brutal enigma—

> 'I bring to life, I bring to death . . .
> I know no more.'[1]

We turn to history. In that realm in which, more than in physical nature, human activity and intelligence have had play, shall we not find something of the supreme plan and purpose which shall assure or encourage our faith? History—what a disappointing and dubious murmur of voices that is! Even if the ages have 'an increasing purpose,' how shall we find in it a purpose that has any real meaning for us? History may be a great drama; the author of it is unknown to the actors and never cares to know them. 'All the world's a stage,' and we, its tragic comedians, play perforce our little parts and pass. But we turn, from nature and history, to the world within us. Here surely, and especially in the realm of conscience, may we find some evidence of the 'living God' who shall be our God. But hardly! The law

[1] Tennyson's *In Memoriam*, lvi.

of conscience within us is a remarkable command and constraint which, as it asserts itself, does indeed suggest a law-giver that is a moral personality; and yet, by itself, I doubt if it takes us incontrovertibly and assuredly beyond a fact and principle of human life—the fact and principle, namely, that what we call morality is, for us, a good and satisfaction and strength, and the opposite is an evil, a source of unquiet, and a weakness. It indeed, as I say, suggests more; but it hardly says more, or, at least, hardly says it in such a way as to be able to maintain itself as a foundation for a sure faith.[1]

Not in nature, then, nor in history, nor even in conscience does the quest of faith find its satisfaction. It has not been said that these disprove the hopes and yearning of faith; that is by no means true. But they do not fulfil them. The wisest of men are agreed about this. I suppose that among 'the masters of those that know,' a higher place as regards these matters—for Shakspere does not deal

[1] Cf. Dr. Rainy's *Delivery and Development of Christian Doctrine*, pp. 37, 38.

with these questions—can hardly be given to any than is to be given to Plato of the ancients, to Dante of the middle ages, to Bacon of the moderns. There is nothing upon which all three are more distinctly agreed than the fruitlessness, or at least the frailty, of the attempt of reason to satisfy the desires of faith from nature and human life. It is, says Bacon, 'in my judgment, not safe.'[1] It is, says Dante, (more than once), 'desiring fruitlessly.'[2] And one of the most pathetic passages in Plato[3] speaks of our having to sail the seas of darkness and doubt on 'the raft' of our understanding, 'not without risk,' he adds, 'as I admit, if a man cannot find some word of God which will more surely and safely carry him.'[4]

[1] *Advancement of learning,* p. 128.
[2] *Purgatorio,* iii. 38. Cf. *Inferno,* iv. 39.
[3] *Phædo,* 85.
[4] The topics referred to in this and the preceding paragraphs have been discussed very briefly from considerations of time. I hope that what has been said will not be taken to mean that one regards nature, history, and moral life as 'godless.' What is said is that they do not enable us to reach a 'living God,' who is the Father of our spirits and recognizes and treats us as His children. If even nature be moral and history progressive, still they, at the most, tell us only of laws, and 'law,' as the ablest of recent Bampton lecturers has said, 'is

THE FURTHER MEANING 113

This utterance of Plato is not only pathetic, but is, to our minds, also suggestive. 'Some word of God that will more surely and safely carry him'—we cannot but associate with such an expression that of the evangelist that 'the word was made flesh and dwelt among us.' Does, then, the fact of Christ mean such a word of God as the quest of faith seeks in vain elsewhere? 'Lord, to whom shall we go?'—that part of the apostle's cry we can understand; but may we go on with him and say, 'Thou hast the words of eternal life'?

We are encouraged to ask this question not merely by apostolic witness, which could not have finally decisive weight with us to-day, but also and much more by the fact that Jesus Himself so often said that the satisfaction of

<small>universal in its action; it does not individualize; it has no equity, no mercy; it does not treat us as persons' (Illingworth's *Personality, Human and Divine,* v.). Newman, in his *Grammar of Assent,* regards conscience as able to carry us further, but, as stated in the lecture, while it suggests more and is a kind of circumstantial evidence for more, it hardly itself really gives us more than a law of life that 'makes for righteousness.' Behind all these declarations of impersonal principles and forces, our individual spirits still seek the Father of our spirits.</small>

the soul's search for God was met in Him. I shall not refer to passages such as, 'He that hath seen Me hath seen the Father,' which might raise exegetical and critical discussion. There is at least one saying in the Synoptics which serves our purpose, and in the view of Beyschlag it 'possesses the highest guarantee of genuineness as belonging to the original collection of Logia.'[1] When Jesus said that all things were given Him of the Father, and that 'No man knoweth the Father except the Son' (that is Jesus Himself), or 'he to whom the Son will reveal Him,'[2] He virtually said three things. He recognized that the object of the quest of faith was the Father—the living, loving God. He declared, as we have seen that Plato and Dante and Bacon declared, that man could not reach it. But, lastly, He affirmed that He had satisfied this quest, and that others could through, but only through, Him be satisfied also. He, who was the greatest Master of religion the world has ever known, at once thus appreciated

---

[1] *Neutestamentliche Theologie*, i. iii.
[2] S. Matt. xi. 27; S. Luke x. 22.

man's position in the quest of faith and also regarded it as met in and by Himself. Here is no waiting, like Plato, for a surer word; here is the assurance of the truth itself. And surely we already have found enough in Jesus to make us ready to listen to Him when He speaks thus.

When we consider what there is in the fact of Christ that has a meaning of assurance for faith, the essential thing we find is this—that Jesus is supernatural. I use the word, as lawyers say, without prejudice, and in its strictly grammatical sense. What I mean is that He is not to be accounted for by the forces that make human nature as we know it. It is really impossible reasonably to deny this. I shall not raise here the question of what are called the miracles, not from any desire to shirk the question—the purely historical evidence that Jesus rose from the dead seems to me really quite unanswerable—but because it is rather a question of presuppositions about God and Nature, to discuss which would lead us too far afield. But if His miraculous works are made subject of debate, His character attests ever more emphatically that Jesus was a supernatural person. It is, as Tennyson once said, 'more wonderful than the greatest miracle.'[1] The one fact of His sinlessness suffices. That His sinlessness is historically a fact and cannot be an imagining we have already found reason to be assured. It is admitted to be a fact by a great many persons who are above suspicion of a dogmatic bias which prejudices their judgment. Professor Orr, who delights in appealing to the Germans, names [2] among those who are constrained to admit it adherents of the Hegelian school like Daub, Marheineke, Rosencranz, Vatke; mediating theologians of all types like Schleiermacher, Beyschlag, Rothe, and Ritschl; liberal theologians like Hase and Schenkel; and so decided an opponent of the miraculous even as Lipsius. Lists of authorities are a weariness to the flesh rather than illuminative to the spirit, but these names are not without impressiveness when one realizes what is the subject-matter of their common admission. For, disguise it as you may, sinlessness is

[1] *Memoir*, p. 273.
[2] *Christian View of God and the World*, p. 268.

supernatural. Sin is in human nature as we know it, and where there is no sin there is what is—if not infra-human, as in the case of the beasts—what is supernatural. But let us suppose that even this sinlessness is disputed. That Jesus is a supernatural person is still brought home as a personal conviction and impression, a thing of which he is sure, to any man to whom the living spirit of Jesus is such a power as has been already described in life and character. Such a man needs to read neither the claims of Jesus nor the concessions of German critics; he has the witness in himself. As he finds Jesus the principle and potency of a new life that is stronger than all the old forces within him, he argues immediately and unhesitatingly, as was argued long ago, that 'if this man were not of God, He could do nothing.' What the expression 'of God' precisely means we are hardly yet in a position to say. But it means at least this—that there is manifested in Jesus a power greater than the natural forces in human life. Here is a unique fact and which justly we call supernatural. Here is a fact of unique significance for the quest of faith: this supernatural fact will tell us something over and above all other phenomena about the great question to which we seek an answer. The answer of Nature we have read; here is a fact supernatural which we have still to read.

This, then, is the position we have reached—that among the facts of the world, whose voice in answer to the question of faith is so insufficient, has appeared this fact of Christ which has a quite peculiar significance just because it cannot be classified with the other facts of history, but is over and above them—a fact by itself and transcendent. Its meaning, then, is a final word, and is not to be qualified or canceled by the apparent meaning of subordinate facts. All facts are subordinate to the fact of Christ who has shown Himself to be greater than such tremendous facts as sin and death.[1] Therefore to this fact the human spirit turns in its quest of faith for its final answer,

[1] I refer here primarily to that spiritual life after His departure from earth which has already been described; but, if this be admitted, the recorded physical victory over the tomb obtains a certain congruousness, and, with its strong historical support, can hardly be dismissed as a preposterous incredibility.

and it asks what is the character of the power that is in and with the transcendent fact of Christ?

To begin with, it is clearly a spiritual Power. It is not a brutal, meaningless physical compulsion to which, even if we had to yield to it, we as rational spirits would be really superior. It is spirit: it is the highest within our spirits. Its compulsion is ever reason, and to obey it is our freedom. Then, secondly, this Power that is with Jesus is ethical. It is the very Power of holiness and truth and love in our hearts, and all that we know of these things we know through it alone. Lastly, it is personal. By this I mean not so much that it is a personal agent—though of course that is meant too, and it is really implied in a power that is spirit—but rather that it treats us as persons. It does not deal with us *en masse*. It individualizes us and is almost as if made for each of us alone. Whereas in the laws of nature and processes of history we perceive their general meaning but can hardly find in them a meaning for ourselves, in the fact of Christ our difficulty is to express it in general terms, but we are quite sure of what it has meant for our souls.

We describe, then, the Power that is in the fact of Christ as spiritual, ethical, and one that personally takes to do with us. Is not this to name the God we seek? Is not this, most simply and really, to find the 'living God'? What is this 'living God' that our souls desire but a Power precisely such as has been described: a God who, at last we know, is not merely a part of the machine of nature, but the Orderer of it; and is spirit as we are spirit who seek the Father of spirits; who is ethically holy, for we cannot call that God which is not good; who is, finally, one who deals with us as persons and not, as Nature seems to do, but as items in her eternal process? The Power that is with Jesus is surely and really at least the beginning of the faith that there is indeed a 'living God' who is the Friend and Father of our spirits, and our quest for Him, if haply we might find Him, finds its rest in the 'surer word' of the fact of Christ.

And so the fact of Christ is the foundation

of faith in the 'living God.' It is, be it observed, not the teaching or doctrine of Jesus that is this, but the fact of what Jesus Himself is and means.. This distinction is of importance. Faith is based not on the ideas of even the noblest of teachers, but on a fact which declares itself to mean the supreme Word of God. It is not that Jesus has spoken and His words are in the Gospels; it is that God has spoken and His word is in history and experience. The importance of this lies here, that what faith needs is not new ideas, but new facts. As ideas, the central points of Christian faith—such as a trust in the Divine Fatherhood and a hope beyond the grave—are hardly wholly new. Many earnest and noble souls have stretched out their minds towards them. What, then, was lacking for faith? Just that, after all, there were but ideas, speculations, yearnings; and our thoughts on these matters are not the sure measure of what really is. Before the stern, unyielding facts of life and especially before life's final fact of death, how easily such thoughts falter and fail.

> 'Eternal hopes are man's
> Which, when they should maintain themselves aloft,
> Want due consistence: like a pillar of smoke
> That with majestic energy from earth
> Rises, but, having reached the thinner air,
> Melts and dissolves, and is no longer seen.'[1]

Who will assure us, in face of 'the thinner air' that is the breath of death, that these hopes and speculations are the sure 'pillar of cloud' leading us truly to a promised land and are not but a 'pillar of smoke' from the fires of human fancy? A faith thus founded will always be cherishable by certain temperaments—and it is largely a matter of temperament—but it will never really grip the mass of men simply because it is a mere edifice of conceptions insecurely founded on the bed-rock of fact. But it is just this that Christian faith possesses. Its basis, I repeat, is not the ideas of Jesus but the fact. It brings not a new doctrine merely, but new data. It comes not with the theory of a fatherly God, but with a phenomenon, in history and experience, which means that. Now all this is precisely what faith needs. Faith—as

[1] Wordsworth's *Excursion*, iv.

indeed may be said of all truth—is like Antæus in Greek legend, who was invincible when touching mother-earth; and the mother-earth of faith is fact—the fact of Christ.

Perhaps it is well for us to recall here, in thus basing faith on the fact of Christ, that, as we saw, that is a dual fact—one at once of outward history and inward experience. It is on this dual fact that our faith is to be based; in other words, faith has an historical as well as a spiritual witness. There is an influential tendency in our day to receive the latter but discard the former. Teachers such as the late T. H. Green or Dr. Martineau would have faith find its sole authority in the religious consciousness within and not lean on any outward historical revelation.[1] Now it is indeed true— and it had become obscured under apologists like Paley—that no external authority can demonstrate faith. Only within are we really made sure that this is of God. But it does not follow that the inward experience is to be isolated, and that in accepting it we do well to

[1] *Vide* Green's address on *Faith* (*Works* iii.) and Martineau's *Seat of Authority in Religion*.

discard the other. As a matter of fact the inward experience, as has already been said, cannot always, when isolated, maintain itself. It really is not an assured, established witness. Now the Christian assertion here is that God has spoken to men in two corroborating ways —the witness of the historical Christ confirming and thus assuring (not, as Green implies, superseding) the witness within. This was certainly the method of Jesus Himself; as Canon Gore says, He 'undoubtedly intended religious belief to rest on a double basis.'[1] It is precisely this historical corroboration which is needed not to create—for that it cannot do— but confirm faith within us and to assure us we are not mistaken. The outward and inward witness about Christ interlock. The historical seals the spiritual; the spiritual signs the historical. On the complete fact of Christ—the fact that is alike in history and in experience inexplicable except as meaning the living God —faith stands.

It is not necessary that we should discuss

[1] *The Incarnation of the Son of God* (Bampton Lecture, 1891), p. 57.

the varied contents of faith, for obviously if Jesus be the word of God to Man, that includes everything. If God have spoken and have so spoken that 'sufficeth us.' It does not indeed show us everything, but it shows us the one thing we need to know—the *character* of God. God is the God who sent Jesus. Given that as an axiom, faith can work out anything. Take, for example, immortality. Christian faith has no demonstration that death does not end all. But, assured about the character of God, it knows who is the keeper of the keys of the grave, and it can trust its dear ones to Him with calm hope. How far is that better than trying, as spiritualism does, to pick the lock! The character of God is the question in all questions of faith, and when that has been answered faith is at rest about everything.

May we then, now, lay down the pen and say we have stated comprehensively, however slightly, the meaning of the fact of Christ for faith? It is an impossibility. Again we have raised questions that impel us further. We have found that Jesus cannot be truly described or accounted for in the terms of merely mundane phenomena. We say He is, in some unique sense, 'of God.' He was more than a man as we know men. All this must be explicated. Sooner or later we must say what it means. It is obvious that, despite all that has been said, we have still to say with definiteness and finality what this growingly profound fact of Christ is.

II. 'AND THE WORD WAS GOD.'

The question that is now before us stands out like the Matterhorn seen from the valley below. It towers above us to dizziness; but at the first glance you see the summit. The question before us is this: If Jesus be more than a man—in His own consciousness, His sinlessness, His immortal personal presence and power, His mighty works, His significance —what then shall we say of Him? There is only one answer to this question. It is an answer which is not incredible—utterly, wildly incredible—only because it is simply inevitable alike to logic and to religion.

The rational or logical side of the argument can be stated very briefly. If Jesus was more than a man, as we know men, shall we then say that He was a prodigy—superhuman and demi-divine? To state such a position is to expose it. It is true to the data about Christ neither in history nor in experience, and at the same time it raises insuperable objections to itself. In Jesus are to be found things characteristic of a man, and also things—such as His claim to forgive sins or His power to create a new moral self—characteristic of God; but there is nothing about Him characteristic of a being neither man nor God. And the objections to admitting into our thought such a being are too obvious to need emphasis. Demi-divinity is simply a relapse into heathenism. This Arian, or quasi-Arian, view of Jesus has absolutely nothing to say for itself historically or experimentally, and has everything against it philosophically. It is a Christ which no reader of the Gospels would recognize, and in which, as T. H. Green—whom, having named lately to differ from him, I wish to name now with regard and gratitude—says, 'no philosopher who had outgrown the demonism of ancient systems could for a moment acquiesce.'[1] This should be fairly and fully faced. I think there is just ground of complaint when, for example, Keim describes Jesus as 'superhuman miracle,'[2] or Channing says he 'believes Jesus Christ to be more than a human being,[3] and there they leave the matter. One complains of this not in the orthodox but in a purely intellectual interest. These are meant to be serious and exact expressions, or they are not. If they are not seriously and exactly meant, they are intellectually unworthy evasions of the great problem of Christ. If they are serious and exact, they involve—let this be clearly understood—a position for which history has not the smallest support and philosophy has only utter repudiation.

If this be so, what then? There is only a *dernier ressort*. It was reached at a very early stage of Christian thought by a writer of inspired insight who seized his pen and, without argument or explanation, wrote: *the Word was God.* The critical penetrativeness of that writer

[1] *Works*, iii. 172.
[2] *Geschichte von Jesu von Nazara*, Eng. trans., iii. 662.
[3] *Works*, iv. 160.

is too little recognized. He overleapt centuries of controversy. He saw at the first glance, what all history has abundantly demonstrated, that all intermediate compromises, such as the Arian, were neither historically nor logically tenable, and that, therefore, the issue was clean and clear between mere humanity and very Deity. With that issue direct before him, he wrote, not so much the best or highest, but the *only* description of Jesus that he could write. As a Christian, he could not describe Christ as mere man; nor can we. As a thinker he could not describe Him as an intermediate divinity; nor can we. If then he was to write at all he could write but one thing, and if we are to say at all what Christ is, we can say but that one thing too. It is, I repeat, saved from being quite incredible only by being quite inevitable.

I have indicated this logical argument briefly, and therefore, doubtless, very insufficiently, but I do not propose to dwell on it further because, after all, this is driving faith at the point of the bayonet, and spiritual truth is not so reached with reality and certainty. But the Divinity of Jesus is not only a logical conclusion to which we are forced, but is in the very woof of Christian experience. The Christian as a Christian is profoundly involved in it and committed to it.

That by which the Divinity of Jesus is seen to be not a mere logical addendum to Christianity but an integral part of Christianity itself is simply these meanings of the fact of Christ which we have been discussing. What the Christian man finds he receives from Jesus is not simply teaching about God, but is a life and power that are of God Himself. He finds in the fact of Christ all he looks to find in God. As he reads the definition of eternal life as ' to know Thee (that is, God) and Jesus Christ whom Thou hast sent,' he is quite unable religiously to maintain the distinction between the two. He finds God not beyond Christ, but in Him. In the very human life and person of Jesus we find not only a human life and person that direct us to a higher source of power; we find already there the presence and power of what declares itself to be not less than God Himself. When Jesus deals with us and works within us, He does what only God can do. All

THE FURTHER MEANING 131

Christian experience is nothing if it is not this. And if this be so, then, again, we can only in one way say what Jesus is. As Herrmann aptly puts it, 'when we confess His Deity, we simply give Him His right name.'[1] What other name can we give to one who is for us and in us what assuredly only God can be? This is the really Christian meaning of the Divinity of Christ. The dogmatic definitions of the symbols are quite secondary to this. There is no reality in your assertion of the dogma of the Divinity of Jesus unless you mean that for you Jesus is that which only God Himself can be. If He is not this, the orthodox formularies are mere verbiage. If He is this, you cannot but give Him 'His right name,' and though possibly with considerable stumbling at Athanasian or other expressions—rightly to judge of which requires an adequate recollection of their historical conditions—you surely may in words call Him that which in fact He is.

Moreover, all deep and honest Christian life

---

[1] *Der Verkehr des Christens mit Gott,* Eng. trans., p. 112. Some of the expressions in this paragraph are suggested by Herrmann.

goes on upon this foundation. It goes on if we take Jesus to be not only a Friend, or Teacher, or Leader, but, in the most strict and inward sense, our Lord. That Lordship of Jesus obtains over the very prerogatives of personal life. Our hearts, our wills are to be His; our consciences reserve no rights before Him whose authority is our last moral appeal. In actual life, indeed, this completeness of surrender is far from being realized, but it is, in idea, inseparable from Christianity. Now, all this is a relationship utterly intolerable to be given to any save One. It it the surrender of all self-respect and manhood, intellectually or morally, to render it to any man. It is, however, a relationship entirely proper to render towards God,—towards Him alone. If, then, this be the relationship towards Jesus which is the very constituent of Christian life, it surely again appears that to confess His Divinity is only to give its 'proper name' to that of which all Christian life is a practical confession. It comes—to put it more briefly—to this. We cannot be Christians unless we will say to Jesus, most literally and unreservedly, 'My

Lord.' But we simply ought not and must not say that to any creature. If we say 'My Lord' we should be able to add with the honest Apostle, 'My God.' The Christian who will not maintain his Lord's Godhead must find it hard to maintain his own self-respecting manhood.

This, then, is the all but incredible but wholly inevitable conclusion to which we are brought —that Jesus means God.[1] As reason cannot receive Jesus as a demi-god, and as religion cannot regard Him as merely an intermediary revelation, we, who say unalterably that He is more than a man, must go on to say: 'and the Word was God.'

The idea is so utterly staggering and overwhelming—that is, if one in the least thinks of it—that it is difficult to know what it means to believe it. Even when one admits its logical sequence from the historical facts, and its essential admission in all Christian life and ex-

[1] Of course I do not intend this expression in merely the Ritschlian sense that Christ, having for us in religion the value of God, may be *estimated* by us as God. The historical-logical argument is to be combined with the religious, and corroborates the latter's judgment as a fact.

perience, still one feels that such knowledge is too high for us, and we cannot attain to it. Some of the difficulties that are presented to us about it are indeed to be boldly resisted, and even resented. For example, we are sometimes reminded in this connection that we no longer live in pre-Copernican days. This planet, which men used to believe was the center of the universe, and its inhabitants, therefore, at least possibly, the apple of its Creator's eye, we now know to be but a speck amid infinite systems of worlds; and we are, therefore, scornfully asked if it be not but an insanity to imagine that the Infinite Cause whose universe is in endless space has taken the likeness of the creatures of one of the most infinitesimal of His worlds, and has 'dwelt among us.' Now, this is simply an attempt to terrorize the imagination, and is not to be yielded to. We know little or nothing of the rest of the universe, and it may very well be that in no other planet but this is there intelligent and moral life; and, if that be so, then this world, despite its material insignificance, would remain the real summit of creation. But even if this be not so, still man remains man—a spiritual being, capable of knowing, loving, and glorifying God. Man is that, be there what myriads of worlds there may; and is not less than that, though in other worlds were also beings like him. There is therefore a spiritual interest at stake in this small world, and it is therefore not a small world to a God who knows the true proportionate value of the material and the moral. 'Is then,' asks Tertullian, 'the Incarnation unworthy of God?' and he justly replies that 'it is in the highest worthy of God, for nothing is so worthy of God as our salvation.'[1] When Mr. Spencer asks us if we can believe that 'the Cause to which we can put no limits in space or time, and of which our entire solar system is a relatively infinitesimal product, took the disguise of a man,'[2] he may think he is giving us an imposing conception of God; but no conception of God is less imposing than that which represents Him as a kind of millionaire in worlds, so materialized by the immensity of His possessions as to have lost the sense of the

[1] *Adv. Marcion*, ii. 17.
[2] *Ecclesiastical Institutions*, 704.

incalculably greater worth of the spiritual interests of even the smallest part of them.

And yet, though we may repel objections of this kind, the essential difficulty of, with reality, believing in the Incarnation remains. Even a successful argument for it hardly establishes it in our minds as a fact. There is but one thing that will meet this, only one thing that enables us to say not merely 'I cannot deny it,' or 'I admit it,' but—what is a great deal more—'I believe it.' That one thing is to perceive the need for it. So much is this the case, that I will say you cannot with reality apprehend the Incarnation as a fact unless you see, to some degree, a *raison d'être* for that fact. It appeals to us as a truth only when it appeals to us as a divinely necessary truth. And thus if we are to receive with reality this stupendous meaning of the fact of Christ we must ask the meaning of that meaning. We must ask *Cur Deus homo?*

The answer to this question is the final meaning of the fact of Christ, and must be treated by itself in the next lecture. But, introductory to that and in closing this lecture, one thing may be said of the bearing of the idea of the Incarnation on the meaning of Christ we have just been considering, that, namely, for faith and as a revelation of the Divine character. It is the Incarnation and the Incarnation alone that gives faith its supreme word about God's character—that God is love.

What is love? It is more than a kind interest or generous regard. Love has its essential qualities, and these are sacrifice, unselfishness, the giving of one's own and of oneself. If then we are to call God love, we must be able to say that He is sacrificing and unselfish, generous of His own and unsparing of Himself. Now if the word or messenger or revealer of God be not one with Him, then there is indeed an expression of the Divine interest and regard and care, but not, in the deepest sense, an expression necessarily or clearly of love. It does not show really and essentially a *self*-giving on God's part. But love is just a self-giving. I do not say that in that case God would not be love, but only that His love, as love, has not been really exercised or exhibited towards us. But if Jesus be a Divine Incarnate word, then 'in this was the love of God manifested.' Here is God giving Himself. Here is not the sending of another, but the sacrifice of Himself. Here, then, is a great word for faith. God is not merely good, gracious, recognizing us and helping us; in the most real and essential and literal sense He loves us. How great a word that is—' God loved the world!' 'How many hearts have understood it who have never yet understood what " God created the world " or " God will judge the world " means?'[1] It is now the superb commonplace of Christianity. But nothing enables Christianity to say it quite truly except the Incarnation, for nothing else shows us the real self-giving, the personal unselfishness, the literal love of Almighty God.

[1] From *Thoughts from the Writings of R. W. Barbour* (privately printed).

V

THE FINAL MEANING OF THE FACT

'La foi chrétienne ne va principalement qu'à établir ces deux choses: la corruption de la nature et la rédemption de Jésus Christ.'

PASCAL

V

THE FINAL MEANING OF THE FACT

IF we are now going to ask the meaning of that meaning which we have found in the fact of Christ, it is of some importance that we should once more put before our minds what that fact precisely was. The meaning we have found in Christ is that He is an incarnation of the Divine life and power. If we feel we cannot with reality embrace this in our minds unless we also perceive something of the reason and ground of it, then it is, I say, important here to remember what historically that Incarnation was. Let us again, as everywhere, study the fact of Christ.

Why this is important is that there is a way of thinking about this question which, treating it philosophically and not historically, gives us a solution which is no solution. We are told that the idea of the Incarnation is really involved in the very Being of God and His relations to man. If God be spirit and love, He must ever seek to reveal Himself to beings whom He has made capable of receiving such a revelation, and this consummates itself in the taking of manhood into God. The Incarnation is thus part of the process of the Divine life, and the ground and reason of it are to be found there. This line of thought is very characteristic of Hegel and of all philosophers who seek to construe Christianity in terms of an absolute dialectic. The same tendency appears in theology, and the idea of the 'Gospel of Creation,' as Dr. Westcott calls it [1]—that is 'the promise of the Incarnation which was included in the Creation of man'—has received encouragement from considerable, if not from the greatest theologians.[2] It is a speculative nicety which has much about it that is very attractive at first sight; but its attraction fades when we turn to history. For philosophy is interesting

[1] *Vide* Essay at the close of his *The Epistles of St. John.*
[2] *Vide* a just conclusion in Thomas Aquinas, *Sum. Theol.*, pars III. quest. i. art. 3. (Thomas is a theologian who should be more read than he is in the Protestant Church.)

and valuable only as it deals with the facts of the world, and this way of thinking hardly seriously deals with the historical facts of the case. It is admitted that this Divine self-manifestation reaches its highest in Christ. And what was Christ? *Ecce Homo!* There is a coming of God not simply to man, but to sorrow and shame and suffering, to tears and prayers and a sweat. There is an entering into not only human trouble, but an agony unparalleled and unfathomed. This is the Divine self-manifestation, this the Incarnation we have to ponder. It is not Bethlehem only nor Nazareth, but Gethsemane and Calvary. It is not a philosophical idea of an Incarnation, but the historical fact of the Incarnation. You have said nothing by saying that self-revelation by becoming man is involved in the idea of God as loving spirit; do you mean that there is involved in God's life *that* self-manifestation which you see in the 'man of sorrows'? The question is to be faced. Our philosophy must be a theory of the facts of the case. An honored writer on Christianity says that 'the very idea of God may be seen to contain that relation to humanity which is expressed in the person of Christ.'[1] What is that relation? Becoming man? That is but a shallow way to state the facts. It was becoming *that* man—that 'man of sorrows,' that 'thorn-crowned man.' I look at that man. I see His infinite sadness in the upper-room. His agony and sweat in the garden; I hear His 'Father, if it be possible,' His 'My God, My God!' And I ask, is this relation to humanity in 'the very idea of God'? Surely, whatever philosophical reflections may be made about an Incarnation idea, we shall not pretend that these explain the facts of *the* Incarnation. Face the history and there is more to be said. The reason and ground of that so sweet and beautiful, but, in the end and essentially, so awful and mysterious Incarnation are still to seek.

Whether or not we shall ever find the more that is to be said and be able to say it, the line along which we must seek it is made clear for us by Jesus Himself. At the impending of the

[1] Principal Caird's *Fundamental Ideas of Christianity*, ii. 102.

THE FINAL MEANING

very crisis of the dark side of His life, He said —and I do not suppose that the authenticity of the words of institution at the Last Supper are seriously questioned—that His blood was shed 'for the remission of sins.' The word is a key and suffices. It would be only perversity of mind not to use it. The meaning of the Incarnation—I say of *the* Incarnation—is to be found in the fact of sin. Jesus said so and that is enough.

Ah! what a problem this is we have set ourselves if for light upon it we have to turn to what is itself of all problems, the darkest, most difficult, most despairing! And, moreover, this to which we are directed is of all topics, that which our whole nature most dislikes to face; we shall dispute its facts, discount their significance, and, above all, deny their personal application. Let us therefore again say to ourselves that it is Jesus Himself who forces those who would understand Him to follow this line; let us recognize from Him that we cannot fully state the meaning of Christ if we will not frankly study this matter of sin.

1. The Reality of Sin

The study of sin is, if it is to be really serious and effective, a study of oneself. Nothing is more easy than to bring in a charge of universal sinfulness against humanity in general, and to substantiate that alike by facts and by the witness of even non-Christian authorities. 'Sin is common to all men,' says one of the Greek tragedians.[1] 'We have all sinned,' says a Roman moralist.[2] And modern literature—not least, modern fiction—is full of the same confession, and indeed has often to defend itself from the charge of being repulsive and immoral by saying that it is only depicting what life is. But such a general impeachment of humanity as sinful makes hardly any impression on the conscience. It is like the 'all men are mortal' of our logic-books, which we all admitted as a major premise but which never made us in the least realize that we should die. Sin is, like death, not seriously realized except as a personal fact. We really know it only when we know it about ourselves. The word

[1] Sophocles' *Antigone*.
[2] Seneca's *De Clementia*.

'sin' has really no serious meaning to a man except when it means that he is a sinful man.

If then a general impeachment of humanity is not enough to show an individual man his personal sinfulness, what is it that will do this? The answer is that Jesus Christ does it. When a man by his self-indulgence in wickedness has got his life into misery, that may make him realize that evil is a real thing and that he has played the fool; but even this is hardly a conviction of sin. And while in a man's conscience there is what might formulate the charge to him, still even that often fails because it easily becomes deadened and sered and apparently incapable of bringing home its charges against us. It is Jesus Christ who gives a spiritual edge to life's judgments and revives the voice of conscience within us. He Himself says His own spirit is that which convinces men of sin. Let us not think that in studying what sin is we are wandering away from the bright and beneficent fact of Christ. It is in and by facing this fact that we have to confess that we have sinned.

For when a man lets the meaning of Christ

really fully and fairly shine upon his life then it says to him three things about sin.

The first is this: that one has seen and known the better and has chosen and done the worse. The charge, if only we will face it, cannot but go home. We have seen and known the better. Not only the fact of Christ—which, as we saw in an earlier lecture, is a fact of more than bare history—but also life and nature, have again and again brought the issues before us, and we cannot say that, like the brutes, we have had no knowledge of the better way of life. But we have chosen and done the worse in thoughts and words and acts. We know this not in a general sense but concretely and particularly, and not as an occasional or exceptional thing, but as a characteristic of our lives. We recall last year or last week or yesterday, and we name that evil habit or unkind word or selfish act or base thought. We take one form of sin —some besetting sin. We begin to count how often we have yielded to it. We find the number is more than that of the hairs of our head. Our whole past life seems to have been lived for that sin; our whole character to have been

THE FINAL MEANING 149

a companionship with it; our whole nature to have made itself its home. I am not speaking of a notoriously wicked man nor, necessarily, of what are called grosser vices. Let the average man, who has never let Jesus Christ deal with his conscience about the facts of his life, review the last year of it with a mind and heart quite open to all that we have been finding in that fact, and will he not find that his dominant and deepest note, his daily habit of thought or life, his thousand-times repeated characteristic has been, not a noble loving and choosing of the highest when he saw it, but some worldly 'lust of the eyes' or sensual 'lust of the flesh' or—perhaps the most common of all—petty 'pride of life' which he did not blush to yield to even daily, but which it is a shame to him to discover now and to confess even to himself?

This develops into something more—the second thing that the spirit of Jesus brings home to us about sin. It is a thing so individual and personal that it is best stated in the first person. He makes me feel that at least in *me* all this is without excuse; in other words, that I am not only sinful, as all men probably are, but also culpable and guilty with many and special aggravations. This I cannot say in the same way of others; indeed, I often feel there may be and are a hundred excuses for them. I therefore cannot out and out condemn others without Pharisaism. But there is no arrogance in my judging myself. No doubt I have had my temptations too, in circumstances without and temperament within, but I cannot find in these any escape from the charge of being a culpably guilty man. For two reasons I cannot. In the first place, whatever circumstances or temperament may have brought, I have not only done evil but liked to do it. This love of it, which often created the desired circumstances and cherished the suitable temperament, is a fact which I know about my own heart but which I cannot in the same way know of any other man's heart, and it makes me condemn myself in a way in which I can condemn no other. And, in the second place, I know another thing about myself that I know about no one else. I know the chances I had of the better choice and the better way. I knew the special reasons and arguments, arising out of just my experience in life, which should have made me a good man. I recall this mercy and that other in my upbringing, this warning and that in my life's discipline, this call to thought, that appeal to everything worthy in me and so on. I begin to count up these things which are things I know nothing about in my neighbor. And thus I find myself, apart from any general impeachment of humanity or any charge against any other man—I find that at least I have been, in a peculiarly inexcusable and shameful way, a sinful man. And so is it that the very principle on which I cannot judge others is one on which I must judge myself. What that principle is was never better stated than by Burns—

> 'What's done we partly may compute,
> But know not what's resisted.'[1]

It is true; and I will not judge, say, the sad life of Burns himself. But the plea cuts both ways. In myself I know 'what's resisted.' I know the grace I have resisted. And therein I judge myself, and feel, as Bunyan says, that 'every one has a better heart than I have.'[2] Thus, to

[1] *Address to the Unco Guid.*
[2] *Grace Abounding,* 84. Readers of this book will re-

quote another great English writer who often deals with this subject, 'God has given no one any power of knowing the true greatness of any sin but his own, and therefore the greatest sinner that every one knows is himself.'[1] This is strictly true; and this is how every man who has learned from the spirit of Jesus Christ that his has been a sinful life, calls himself with the Apostle, for the clearest reasons, ' The *chief* of sinners.'

All this leads to a third thing. We condemn ourselves because we know ourselves. But Jesus, of whom the woman of Samaria said that 'He has told us all things that ever we did,' makes us realize with a new seriousness that Another knows us too. That other is no mere human judge.

'But what will God say?'[2]

—the living, holy, personal God of whom just Jesus has made us so sure. Is His judgment

member how Bunyan feels what is said above when he begins to compare himself with other sinners—David, Peter, and even Judas.

[1] Law's *Serious Call,* chap. xxiii.
[2] Browning's *Worst of it.*

THE FINAL MEANING 153

laxer and less serious than our judgment of ourselves? He is indeed good, but 'He shows His love of good by His hate of sin.' What will He say? God cannot regard us as other than we really are. And what is it that we really are? We have just been discovering that. We are persons who knew the better and did the worse, and that without excuse, with the deepest aggravations and despite a thousand reasons and restraints that should have kept us. If God be God, if God be morally worthy to be God, what is and must be His relation towards such? Our religion comes to an unhappy pause. Our search for God, if haply we might find him, is clouded with a dark apprehension lest we should too really and nearly find Him or He find us. Our cry of 'My soul is athirst for the living God; when shall I appear before the presence of God?' becomes the other cry of 'Whither shall I flee from His presence?' We dislike the thought of God. We avoid the thought of the future. Our desire and effort become to forget God,

[1] Tertullian's *adv. Marcion*, iv. 26.

and to evade such things, as death, that remind us of Him. 'Thus conscience doth make cowards of us all.'

Are these unworthy and degrading thoughts, akin to the gloomy terrors of the heathen on whom the beneficent light of Christ has not dawned? It is easy to call them such, but they are not. The meaning of the fact of Christ for faith indeed dispels all fears about God that arise from the thought of Him as wicked and unjust and unholy. But these solemn apprehensions which arise in the mind of the man who perceives that he is a sinful man come not from the thought of God as wicked and unjust and unholy, but on the very contrary, from the thought of Him as righteous and just and holy—in other words, from a true, not an untrue, thought of what God is. From these apprehensions many things would deliver us, but these things are the spirit of unbelief, the narcotics of pleasure, the *optare non esse Deum*.[1] The fact of Christ does not treat these apprehensions as morbid and foolish dreams. He awakens them and deepens them and makes

[1] 'The wish that God did not exist.'

our consciences feel them to be eternal moral truths. He convinces us not only 'of sin,' but also 'of judgment.' And—without the smallest morbidness or superstition, but only with moral sanity and seriousness may it be asked—wherewithal shall we, who cannot stand before our own consciences, stand before the Searcher of hearts and not be overwhelmed? *Nur das Vollkommne vor Gott vorstehen kann.*[1] The question may be evaded. It may be evaded by a refusal seriously to think what on the one hand God is, and on the other we are. It may be evaded. But it remains.

It thus would appear that the problem of sin is deepening and darkening. It is something far more than the moral problem of character. As we have already seen, there is a problem of character. Evil has its results in bad habits, sinful disposition, and bears fruit in many moral and even physical consequences in this life. But it appears this is not all the meaning of evil in man. For it bears other

[1] Schleiermacher's *Der Christliche Glaube,* ii. ('Only the perfect can stand before God.')

than these temporal fruits, and has eternal consequences towards God. Here is a matter calling for more than we found in the fact of Christ when we were discussing the first meaning of that fact. The problem of immorality—that is, man's character viewed only by itself—is a small thing compared to the problem of sin—that is, man's character viewed *sub specie æternitatis* and under the condemnation of God.

What a sad confusion seems to have overtaken us in our investigations! The fact of Christ that had opened to us such happy and hopeful prospects in the spheres of character and of faith, has now darkened the day of its own heralding and has developed meanings that seemingly destroy both hope and happiness. For think what is meant by God's condemnation of sin—of us who are sinners. To say it means punishment is only to say the same thing in another word, but what is punishment but simply displeasure in operation? It means far more than punishment. There is no good of which it does not mean the loss; there is no hope of good of which it does not mean the abandonment. Is it to this that after all Jesus has brought us? Is the fact of Christ like one of Heine's poems that begin with thoughts of beauty and of peace which, in the last verse, they shatter by some word of bitterness and despair?

But this is not the last word of Jesus Christ about our sin and about God's view of it. We must read on.

II. THE PROBLEM OF FORGIVENESS

The further word that is to be found in the fact of Christ concerning sin and God's view of it can be stated very shortly. It does not admit of dispute. The light and liberty that Jesus brings with Him wherever He is received honestly and cordially mean—despite all that has just been said—that we are being treated by God *not* with displeasure and condemnation but with favor and approval. The word of the Gospel and the experience of the Christian man are a delusion if this be not so. In the fact of Christ we are assuredly called to a glad confidence towards God and a happy expectancy not of evil but of good, and we have the sure conviction that He is not against us, but is and eternally will be for us. Jesus has simply misled our hearts if the Christian, finding all this in the fact of Christ, may not rest upon it as final and true about God.

It is obvious that only one word solves the paradox thus created, and reconciles this grace and assurance on God's part towards us with that displeasure and condemnation which the same fact of Christ made us feel must also be in God towards sinners. Observe how these two apparent contradictions are to be reconciled. We are not to admit one into our minds by simply ousting or forgetting the other. In saying that God receives us and welcomes us, we must also and at the same moment remember that we are full of sin and God's face is set against sin. These contraries must be fairly reconciled, and, I say, there is obviously only one word that reconciles them. That word is forgiveness. In forgiveness is contained the reality of sin, else there were nothing to forgive; in it is contained also the reality of God's free favor to us, else we were not forgiven. We are really sinful men; we are really received and welcomed by God. These two facts put together can mean only that God has forgiven our sins.

The conclusion may seem a very simple one. It is not a simple conclusion. Here we have reached the very crux of the fact of sin— namely, the problem of the forgiveness of sin. That God forgives is something we are apt to take as almost axiomatic. Let us think a little carefully and exactly what it means for God to forgive sins.

We naturally assume that it means for Him just what it means for us, and that there is involved in the Divine forgiveness of our sins just what is involved in one man forgiving an injury done to him by another. Thus, Priestley—a most honest, truth-seeking man—says that 'it is required of us that if our brother only repent we should forgive him even though he should repeat his offence seven times a day; on the same generous maxim, therefore, we cannot but conclude that the Divine Being acts towards us.'[1] The conclusion appears at first sight, undeniable, unless, as Socinus says— from whom the argument is taken—'we wish

[1] *Corruptions of Christianity*, i. 151.

to concede less to God than is conceded to men themselves'[1] But a more careful reflection will, I think, show us that it is a conclusion containing an utterly inadequate conception of God, and that the question is one of conceding not less to God than to men, but infinitely more. One is inclined to reply to Socinus and Priestley in the words which Luther once used to Erasmus in their discussion on free-will: 'Your thoughts concerning God are too human.'[2]

Consider the essential difference in the relations of God and of man to the fabric of morality. We are merely private individuals, and our passing over of our injuries, which are but personal wrongs, does not in the least degree involve that that law by which, in an ethical world, evil and its due reward are, as Plato says, 'riveted together'[3] is abrogated or compromised. The moral fabric of the universe does not depend on us, nor is it altered by what we do. Indeed, it is only as private individuals that, in general, we can forgive, and if our

[1] *Prælect. Theol.*, xvi. The objection is of course much older still; it is mentioned by Anselm.
[2] Luther's *De Servo Arbitrio*, sect. xv.
[3] *Phædo*, ix.

forgiveness would have social or public effects endangering moral order in the community, then it may be impossible. Now, Almighty God is not a magnified private individual. He is the very source and center of the ethical order of the universe, and it does depend on Him. Thus the just and ethically true connection between evil and its due judgment is abrogated if He abrogate it; and that means ethical disorder and ethical chaos and the world no longer a morally constituted world. Such forgiveness would be on God's part, what it is not on ours, an act involving moral anarchy. It is of real importance that this essential difference between God and ourselves in this matter be recognized. A modern American theological writer insists repeatedly that this matter of forgiveness is 'not a matter of relation to law or to government; it is primarily and essentially a matter of the relations between persons, God and man,' and that 'it is the personal relation that needs to be set right, and it is through being right with God that men are to be made right with the government of God.'[1] The dis-

[1] *Outline of Christian Theology*, by W. N. Clarke, D.D., New York, p. 322.

tinction seems to me of no essential value—it may have a use as a check to abstractly forensic forms of speech—for the law and the person of God are one. God *is* the ethical order. In Him, as Dr. Dale says, 'the law is alive.'[1] It is, therefore, of no essential meaning to speak of a 'personal relation to God' in forgiveness as if that were 'not a matter of relation to law.' I repeat that God is the moral law. And because He is and we are not that, there is no just comparison between forgiveness in us and in Him. With us, indeed, what we call forgiveness is rather a forgetting of our injuries; but there can be no mere forgetfulness in God's forgiveness. If the just and eternal ethical order that is the very foundation of a moral universe rivets together sin and its due reward, how can He who is that very order, separate them and yet be its God? Forgiveness is to man the plainest of duties; to God it is the profoundest of problems.

Is it not, indeed, as Dr. Chalmers used to say, 'a problem fit for a God?' It is no petty question of personal unwillingness to forgive,

[1] *The Atonement*, Lect. ix.

or of personal vindictiveness. It is a question of the ethical order of the universe—an order that is of the very being of God. What is the problem? It is to declare in one breath that the wages of sin is death, and also that we who are sinners are heirs of eternal life. It is to save men, who, by the ethical order of a moral universe, are condemned and yet at the same time save the ethical order that condemns them. It is to be eternally just and also the eternal justifier of the unjust. There is the problem. No man has any such problem presented to him in forgiving another man. But when God would forgive us, *He* has to face it. It is a problem for God, and 'a problem fit for a God.'

All this means that in the end the question of the forgiveness of sins is not simply a 'whether'—one of inclination merely—but is a 'how.' The problem falling to God and 'fit for a God' is to find the *way* of forgiveness. There can be little doubt as to where that is to be sought. We turn again to Him who called Himself 'the Way'—to the fact of Christ. All through our discussion, I have sought that we should never for long be out of sight of history. The compass of reasoning has its great uses, but it easily gets out of gear; facts are the infallible stars by which the voyager seeking truth must ever regulate his course. The facts about Jesus on the matter that now is before us are plainly—as I have said He Himself connected them—the facts about His death; and by that is meant, as Professor Denney describes it, ' the experience which the Son of God anticipated in Gethsemane and underwent to Calvary.'[1] To this, then, we turn.

It is to turn to the most profoundly perturbing spectacle in history. We look at Him whom we have raised in our faith to a very Deity, whose every feature we have come to regard with an adoration, whom we have found among men not so much first as incomparable and only—we look at Him in what a great man[2] touchingly and truly called ' the last trial,' and we find Him, at the prospect of His death, in an agony. That sweat of blood, that broken prayer, that falling on His face again

[1] *Studies in Theology*, p. 105.
[2] Mr. Gladstone.

THE FINAL MEANING 165

and yet again; that overmastering sorrow and depression, that utter dread and horror, that inexpressible disquietude and anxiety, and terrible consternation of spirit [1]—what does all this mean? We scorn indeed the baser sort of unbelievers who, with all disregard of the decency which any martyr has a right to expect in his hours of suffering, have pointed a taunting finger to that figure. In the name of decency, it is not to be mocked; but how can it, in the name of truth, be adored? Is Jesus here the incomparable, the only, even the supreme? We recall the wonderful scene in the prison-cell at Athens when Socrates met his 'last trial' with such calm and such good cheer. We read again the closing pages of the *Phædo;* how beautiful they are! And then we look again at that agonizing figure, and our adoration of Jesus receives a shock. Our minds—dislike it as they may, and resist it as they will—seem forced to admit to themselves that in one thing Jesus is not our perfect example and inspira-

[1] The expression translated in the A.V. 'sorrowful,' 'sore amazed,' and 'very heavy,' are immensely stronger in the original. *Vide* the somewhat full note in Pearson, *On the Creed,* Art. iv. ('Suffered.')

tion. And that single thought has enough in it to alter our whole Christianity.

There is only one thing that saves us from this conclusion, and that is that the comparison out of which it arose be an impossible one. If 'the cup' which Socrates took 'quite readily and cheerfully,'[1] and 'the cup' from which Jesus prayed in an agony to be delivered were alike but death, then (even though the latter's was a more painful and shameful death) the conclusion is inevitable. It is good to say these things plainly to our minds; and if the death of Jesus was just death, we have not given Him His entirely right name when we say He is Divine, nor even His entirely right place when we regard Him as our perfect and complete ideal. But was it just death? Jesus Himself suggests otherwise.

We recall again His saying that His death was 'for the remission of sins.' And we recall what we have been thinking about the meaning of the remission or forgiveness of sins. We saw that forgiveness—that is, God's forgiveness, who alone really ultimately forgives—

[1] *Phædo*, 117.

must include in its meaning a dealing with the whole ethical order by which sin and its due desert are, to use Plato's phrase again, ' riveted together.' It must in no way subvert or compromise this, but on the contrary must respect it, and do all that is right by it.[1] Now Jesus said that His death was ' for the remission of sins.' Then in His death is the doing right by that ethical order which binds together sin and its due desert; then it was that bond (the terribleness of which, we, just because we are forgiven, can only faintly and indeed hardly at all imagine) which tightened at His heart and pressed His brain—the heart that had known no other bond to God but love, the brain that had never thought of Him but with joy. One says these things simply, and the words in which they are said are cold and colorless. But when one really thinks of the realities which the words cover, the mind is overwhelmed. Strange and startling thoughts invade it. That agony of Jesus, as we look on it, ' harrows us with fear and wonder.' Does

[1] This last expression is Principal Rainy's. (Cf. German *genugthun.*)

it find its meaning, not in a human weakness, which though we should never mock it, we could not adore, but in the unprecedented strain of the meeting of human sin and that moral order which condemns sin—that appallingly real and absolutely uncompromising meeting which had to take place somewhere, somehow, if a Divine, an ethically true and ultimate forgiveness was to be? It has not taken place in our lives; that we know. Did it take place then? How, then, would all comparisons between the cup of hemlock and *that* cup be hushed and shamed and awed!

These seem wild, and may seem even monstrous, thoughts, but it is Jesus Himself who suggests them. And the Christian mind—the mind led by that Spirit which was to 'take the things of Christ and show them unto us'— does not recoil from them appalled, but it is sure that they are true. It has no doubt, that is to say, that the meaning of the death of Jesus is His bearing the responsibility for sin in face of the law of God that condemns sin. The Christian man is sure of it not simply because the alternative is, as I have indicated, the affecting of all his Christianity. He is sure of it for another reason. In that death—and let us again remember that that means the whole experience from Gethsemane to the end—the Christian man can recognize something that should be his own but has not been, and, in the evangel come in Jesus, is not to be his own. It brings home what would be his case if he, with all his sins upon his head, 'unhousel'd, disappointed, unaneled,' were brought to face God's law. A dark and dreadful mystery hangs over the Garden and the Cross, but one thing in it all presses home clear—there I might have been and should have been. This is why the Christian heart in all ages—with doubtless varied interpretation, yet with a common experience deeper than its differences—has said, 'He was wounded for our transgressions,' or, 'Who died for us,' or, 'Who loved me and gave Himself for me.' There is nothing or little gained by multiplying words about this. It cannot be said much better or very differently in the end than at the beginning, or by the most learned than by the simplest. It is the 'our,' the 'us,' the 'me' that say it all.

You cannot state this great meaning of the death of Jesus without personal pronouns. When you can use these thus you have said everything. You have found the final meaning of the fact of Christ.

The final meaning of the fact of Christ, then, is that He has opened up 'the way of forgiveness' for us by, on our account, doing right by the ethical order which connects sin and its due desert, and without respect to which a true, ultimate, and Divine forgiveness could not be. Thus He 'reconciles us to God,' who is that ethical order, and on the strength of this, religion as a fellowship and friendship between God and us can begin and go on. Let us note the two pillars on which all this view rests. One is ethical principle, the other historical fact. The principle is that forgiveness in God must not compromise or subvert the order of a moral universe; the fact is the death of Jesus as interpreted by His own words, by the general impression of His life and character and person, and by the consciousness of the Christian man. On these pillars rests the stupen-

THE FINAL MEANING 171

dous phenomenon of what, in theological language, is called the Atonement.

There are many persons who, at this point, stop; that is to say, as it is usually put, they accept 'the fact of the Atonement,' but profess no sort of explanation of it. They say with Coleridge, '*factum est;* and, beyond the information contained in the enunciation of the fact, it can be characterized only by its consequences';[1] or with Butler, in more guarded terms, that 'if the Scripture has, as surely it has, left this matter of the satisfaction of Christ mysterious,' then 'it is our wisdom thankfully to accept the benefit by performing the conditions upon which it is offered on our part, without disputing how it was procured on His.'[2] Now, if what is meant by such language is that we cannot reduce to a final and complete statement the principles involved in the forgiveness of sins through the work of Jesus, then it is all admitted. For to under-

[1] *Aids to Reflection.* There does not seem to be much aid to reflection in the bare enunciation of an impenetrable *factum est.*
[2] *Analogy,* pt. II. ch. v.

stand fully the Atonement were to understand these three things and their ultimate relation to each other—the greatest thing in God, which is His love; the strongest thing in the universe, which is law; and the darkest thing in man, which is sin. These are matters which certainly stretch beyond our comprehension. But if what Coleridge and Butler mean is that we cannot even expect to discern any moral or rational principles in this great fact, that is quite another thing. In this case the Atonement could be in no proper sense a fact for religion. For religious truth is truth that has it in it to be a motive and persuasion and appeal to the life of thinking beings. Its facts, then, cannot be facts impenetrable to thought. They must be luminous, not opaque. To deny this of the Atonement is really to dislodge it from religion and make it a merely algebraical fact. It will indeed ever stretch beyond us into mystery—and it is good for us thereby to be reminded that God's thoughts are 'greater than the measure of our minds'—but it cannot be *merely* a mystery. Its principles, however inexhaustible, must be approachable. To Christian thought and experience they must suggest not the dumb darkness of mystery but the light of rational and moral truth.

It is perhaps reasonable that, having said this, one should add a few words in elucidation of these principles. These lectures are not theological, and it did not seem necessary in connection with either of the other meanings of the fact of Christ to discuss the doctrine, in the one case, of the Holy Spirit, or, in the other, of the Incarnation. In these cases the religious facts had their own sufficient meaning and value. But for various reasons the subject of the Atonement is in a somewhat different position. It cannot have even its purely religious value for us if we are in the dark or in error as to any understanding of it. And, therefore, one may add to what has been said an addendum with some remarks on the spiritual principles that seem to underlie the forgiveness of our sins through the Atonement of Jesus Christ. It must be understood that only the briefest outline is attempted here.

Addendum: The Principles of the Atonement

The work of Jesus Christ in atoning for the sins of men is not a new departure in His life. It is but the carrying out to its bitter end that saving of men which was His aim all through. What, therefore, we should seek in it is not new principles but rather new implications and applications of the ruling principles already discernible in other and less mysterious aspects of His work. And so I begin by asking what is the ruling principle in all Christ's relations to man in His coming to save us?

What that is it is not difficult to discover. It has presented itself all through our investigations of the fact of Christ. Let us recall the first and simplest of the meanings we have found in this fact. When we discussed the meaning of Christ for ethical life and character we discovered that to be more and other than His bequeathing to us a lofty teaching and a supreme example. We found that He gave us of His spirit, which means that, in a wonderful but real way, He Himself entered into and became part of our thoughts and affections and will—part of, in short, ourselves. 'I live, yet not I, but Christ liveth in me.' He is the real name of our better and true self. Something of this is all through characteristic of Christianity, and is distinctive—something that has no pretence to a parallel in Buddhism or Mohammedanism. This is a clear and distinctive element in Christ's saving relation to men, and the principle of it is simply enough stated. It is that of a oneness, an inward unitedness between Christ and humanity. This is the idea expressed by Christ Himself under such a figure as 'I am the vine, ye are the branches,' and St. Paul carries on the same idea by such a figure as that of the head and the members. This spiritual oneness with Christ, who not only comes before us in history but becomes one within us and identical with us—Christ is in a wonderful way identical with a man's best self—is the principle in all His saving relations to men, and Christianity cannot be stated apart from it. And the principle that is at the root of forgiveness is not, I repeat, a new departure, but is a further application of the same idea.

The problem of forgiveness we have seen to be this. God is the source and sustainer of the ethical order of the universe—rather, indeed, is that order—and an ethical order that is truly ethical must condemn sin and 'rivet together' (as Plato said) sin and doom; how then can God forgive a humanity that is sinful? The principle of a oneness between Christ and humanity suggests, in answer to this question, a counter-question, namely: How can God condemn that which has Christ in it? If Christ be one with us, so that God cannot look at us apart from Him, how shall condemnation be God's verdict on us? This is the principle of the Atonement. It is the essential principle in any aspect of Christianity, but it has, in connection with this aspect of forgiveness, new and profound implications and consequences.

Two quotations from two eminent teachers will illustrate the directions in which these lie. There is a famous passage in Luther's *Commentary on the Epistle to the Galatians* in which he applies this idea in one direction with characteristic vividness and force. He represents God as saying to Christ: 'Be thou Peter the denier, Paul the persecutor . . . . briefly, be Thou the person that hath committed the sins of all men.' Then, Luther goes on: 'The law cometh and saith, I find Him a sinner . . . therefore let Him die.'[1] The quotation needs no exposition; there can be no dubiety about Luther's meaning. But another eminent writer on the subject applies the same idea in precisely the opposite way. M'Leod Campbell—whose work on the Atonement, however criticizable in parts, is one of the few books of its kind that command and repay careful study—says in a strain very similar to Luther: 'Let us suppose that all the sin of humanity has been committed by one human spirit . . . and let us suppose this spirit, loaded with all this guilt, to pass out of sin into holiness . . . becoming perfectly righteous, with God's own righteousness.' In such a case, which is 'the actual case of Christ, the holy one of God, bearing the sins of all men,' this righteousness would be, Dr. Campbell thinks, a 'true and proper satisfaction.'[2]

[1] *In loc.* iii. 13.
[2] *Nature of the Atonement*, ch. vi.

In other words, and to contrast this view with Luther's, when 'the law comes' it finds not so much Him—that is, Christ—a sinner and so says He must die, as rather that the sinner is become Christ and so it is satisfied.

All views of the Atonement may be roughly classified according to which of these two directions they take. One class emphasizes Christ's union with us and our sin: 'Him that knew no sin God made sin on our behalf.' The other emphasizes humanity's oneness with what He is: 'by the obedience of one many were made righteous.' Now the most intellectually irritating thing in the world is a false alternative. There is a false alternative when we are invited to pit these views against one another, and choose one of them or the other. Both views must be held; both directions followed. And for this clear reason. The principle is a oneness, a union, between the sinner and Christ. Well, a union just because it is a union, has two complementary aspects and involves two sets of consequences. If Christ and His people are one, that has implications for us in view of what He is, and also implications

THE FINAL MEANING

for Him in view of what we are. The one result follows as much as the other. We must look along the lines suggested by the German doctor and also those suggested by the Scottish. The Atonement, because its principle is a union, has two sides, and *non uno itinere potest pervenire ad tam grande secretum.*[1]

It is the implications in that aspect of this union which Luther emphasized in the quotation given above which are the more unwelcome to many. But to become man surely must include some relation on Christ's part to the position in which man stood. For humanity was in a certain position—the position, namely, of being condemned by the ethical order which connects sin and doom. If Christ became man with a reservation on this point, then He evaded the very point of man's need. But there is no justification for the suggestion of any such reservation. He took upon Him to deliver man. To do so, He became man under the condition that created the need of deliverance, and that is the condition of con-

---

[1] "Not by one way only can we reach to so great a secret."

demnation. By no word or act did Christ disregard that condition or minimize it. On the contrary He accepted it as His condition because it was the condition of the humanity with which He identified Himself. And He then dealt with it. He dealt with it in a great and serious and real way; not seeking to shirk it or subvert it, but doing all that is right by it. And He did right by it by letting all that such a condition had to say be said to Himself. In saying this we must take care not to say more than this. How it works out, and what it precisely meant for Him are not to be unguardedly stated. Expressions such as that God punished Christ or that God was angry with Him are inappropriate, and the latter is—as even Calvin admits [1]—an impossibility. But the things that are clearly to be asserted are two: that the ethical law connecting sin and doom was in no wise suppressed, but was given effect to really and adequately; and that this full and adequate expression of it came upon Him. It has not come upon us; it is part of the evangel that it will not come upon us. But

[1] *Institutio*, II. xvi. 11.

THE FINAL MEANING 181

it has not therefore been canceled. It has had right done by it. If you ask, Where? the answer is to be found in the fact that when Christ became man He accepted the condition in which man stood and its consequences, and He exhausted them on our behalf. Whatever difficulty or mystery is about this, it and it alone upholds an absolutely essential principle in any forgiveness that can be of God—namely, that the ethical order of a moral universe is not thereby compromised. The reality of this identification with us of Him who ' was numbered with the transgressors' that He might make answer on their behalf must be held to, though in this —as indeed in all His relations to us—Christ is more and undertakes more than we can explain.

This is one side of that oneness between Christ and us which is the principle of forgiveness. But it is only one side. All this is fundamental, but not final. It is only one-half of an Atonement. The need of the other side suggests itself immediately. For even granting to the full the facts of Christ making Himself answerable to the ethical order connecting sin and doom, after all, how does that affect me? I am not Christ. He may have made an answer, but that does not make it my answer. If I were He, it were all well; but I am not He. I am still a sinner, and I am answerable still. It is here that the principle of the Christian religion—that of union between Christ and man—approaches us again, and, with its complementary application, completes its evangel of forgiveness.

It comes saying this. Here is Christ who is 'the righteous,' who has done right by all the claims of ethical order that connect sin and doom, and He would now be your true self. As He has identified Himself with *man* as far as man's general relation to God's laws was concerned, so now He calls *men*—individual hearts and wills—to admit Him to a personal union with themselves. This is the call of the evangel of forgiveness. Not to believe any mere fact or doctrine such as Christ died for sins; but to receive, to become one with, in mind, heart and will, the Person who has thus answered for sin. Then, in a real and spiritual sense, is not His answer yours, if you in a real and spiritual sense are He? 'There is therefore no condemnation to them that are in Christ Jesus.' They are identified with the perfect answer to the law connecting sin and doom, because in inward reality they are identified with the Answerer.

Thus our union to Christ—an inward union of mind, heart, will, and life—completes what He did in identifying Himself with our condition, and the result is the gospel of forgiveness. Observe how ethical this gospel is. A spurious evangel of forgiveness that merely rings the changes on what Christ has done till we 'only believe it' may well be open to the charge of not at least necessarily securing for forgiveness an adequate and immediate ethical content. And in evangelical Protestantism, the forgiveness of sins is too often represented as one thing, and Christian morality as another—the latter to be expected to follow the former from, generally, the sense of gratitude. This is a very defective and erroneous manner of stating it. The true way of it is this. Forgiveness is not only because of Christ but in Him.[1] There is no such thing in the gospel as mere forgiveness. There is nothing in the gospel that is separable from Christ. You cannot have forgiveness without having Him, that is, without admitting Him to an inward union with your mind and heart and life. Only thus is His answer yours. But you cannot thus admit Christ to mind and heart and life without admitting the whole business of the moral life. And so morality is no mere addendum to forgiveness. It comes as an imperative and indisputable part of Christ, of whom also forgiveness is an indissociable part. You cannot have this which we are calling the final meaning of the fact of Christ, without having also the first meaning of the same fact,—without finding that He means for you a new life. Christ is not divided.

But while this is to be said, there is something else also to be said. I have tried to say that forgiveness is inseparable from the moral ideal that rises before us, and that it is only by our being inwardly one with the great An-

[1] This is a point greatly insisted upon by Luther.

swerer of the law's claims that His answer is ours. Now our realization of the moral ideal and our union in mind and heart and life with Christ are really but begun. It might therefore seem that our forgiveness is in a merely embryo stage, a state of probation rather than of assured achievement. But this is not the note of the evangel. Whenever we are really united in sincerity of heart and will to Christ, even though it be, as it will be, imperfectly, then, already, His answer to the law of condemnation is ours and that is a finished and complete answer. With our point of contact with Him we find something on which we can take a stand. He *has* redeemed us from the curse of the law. And thus arises, in all true evangelical Christianity, its note of immortal assurance towards God. It is not the dawn of the faint hope of forgiveness in the end. It is a confidence stablished and firm and sure. In our contact with Christ we find also a call, as I have said, to begin and go on with a holy life. But it is a great thing when the Christian man goes forth to that conflict animated with the sense of what his Lord has done for him against his foes, and so fights with the inspiration of a redemption achieved and secure.[1]

These few paragraphs, however fragmentary they may be, must suffice here as a statement of the principles of the atonement for sin through Jesus Christ. It is not to be expected that any statement, even the most elaborate, can be an exposition of the matter finally or shall answer all difficulties about it. It must be remembered that the whole event is essentially and absolutely unparalleled, and that therefore it cannot be brought under general principles. It is unparalleled simply and clearly because its primary condition is unique. That is a oneness between Christ and His people. This is a thing unparalleled in human experience and cannot be reduced under any general categories of friendship or the solidarity of the race or any

---

[1] I venture to think that what this paragraph asserts is at the heart of the evangel, the 'great truth' of which is rather here than, as Canon Gore states, in that 'God deals with us by anticipation.' *(Incarnation of Son of God,* p. 225.) Canon Gore quotes Augustine's well-known expression, that God regards us '*non quales sumus, sed quales futuri sumus,*' which is true, but not so true as its converse. It is a suggestive rather than a scriptural expression.

other. Of no other do we speak as we do of Christ, who is, says a Father, 'our inseparable life';[1] of no other leader or teacher do we say that he and his are, as a great saint and doctor describes Christ and Christians, '*quasi una persona mystica.*'[2] Here is the root principle of the whole matter, and because it is something absolutely unique, the Atonement itself cannot be brought under any final general explanation. And if this unique root principle were remembered, many of the difficulties and objections that are raised on this subject would disappear. The chief and central objection to the whole idea is that there is injustice in it; it is unjust that one should thus bear the sins of another. But are these words 'one' and 'another' quite applicable? Here is really no 'other'; as it is put in an old Scottish catechism—'Christ is not another person from His people properly.'[3] This, if you will, is mystical, and I cannot explain in terms

[1] Ignatius, *Ad Ephes.*, III.
[2] Thomas Aquinas, *Summa*, pars III. quæst. xliii. art. II.
[3] *Craig's Catechism.* A thought also in Thomas Aquinas and Bernard.

any point where God touches man. But the mystery is fact and in that fact is the answer to many an irrelevant and inappropriate charge against the Atonement. Often these arise from the 'illustrations' of persons with unscriptural and inexact imaginations. There can be no illustrations of the Atonement. The Cross is its own interpreter. And if this be so, and is so because of its unique central principle of the oneness of Christ and the Christian, then we shall perceive that the reality of it all is seen best, not from the disputings of the divines, but in the school of the spirit's communion with God. St. Paul deals most deeply with it in his prayers. It is when a man confesses his moral bankruptcy before God and realizes it, that it comes home to his need how the Holy and Harmless One so loved him as to identify Himself with even his condemnation, and has answered on his behalf. To mock at this evangel is the jest of him who never felt the wound. It is a sinner's only religion.

VI

WHAT IS A CHRISTIAN?

Ἐμοὶ γὰρ τὸ ζῆν Χριστὸς καὶ τὸ ἀποθανεῖν κέρδος.
                                                ST. PAUL.

VI

WHAT IS A CHRISTIAN?

WE have now reached a stage at which we may pause and gather up some practical results from the ground over which we have traveled.

In the first place we sought the original data of Christianity, and these we saw to have been, not in a philosophical or ethical system, but in Jesus Christ Himself. We went on to ask how far our religion of to-day could be based on such data, and found that Christ is a fact not only of history but also of present spiritual life and experience—a fact, that is, within the proper sphere of religion. Therefore we went further and inquired what meanings this fact contains for religion, and we found it to hold meanings of the profoundest kind for character, for faith, and for conscience—a new moral life, a real revelation of the living God and an evangel of assured forgiveness. All this is religion, and this religion is Christianity, which we cannot better define than as *the meaning of the fact of Christ.* Indeed, that in that fact are the data of the Christian religion has for its correlate that Christianity is the content of these data—the meaning of Christ.

But after all, to have done all this is not to have done the main thing. After all, the main thing is not to understand Christianity but to be a Christian. The Light must be the life. As Dr. Chalmers—always a great teacher on the moral bearings of any truth—said, our chief business with Christianity is 'to proceed upon it.'[1] We have described this religion; we must not close without considering what is to be done with it. We have been asking what Christianity is; but what is a Christian?

This question must be answered clearly and simply, for to be a Christian is certainly not something abstruse and difficult to understand. On the other hand it must be answered with a just and adequate relation to Christianity as a whole, and not merely in respect to some one point in it. We shall guard ourselves in both

[1] *Lectures on the Romans,* lxxi.

of these directions by remembering what we have found Christianity to be. It is the meaning of Christ. Well, a Christian would then naturally be described as one who is responding to that meaning. I shall explain the word 'responding' more fully presently, but I use it here in preference to any such more usual word as 'believing,' because the latter has come to be associated with merely matters of creed, while, as we have seen, Christ has meanings for life and character as well as, and perhaps even prior to, faculties of intellect. Apart, however, from such explanation, to speak of responding to the meaning of the fact of Christ at once raises a question. It will be said that we have been stating the most stupendous meanings in the fact and meanings that are, to many, surrounded with the utmost intellectual difficulty. Is it to be said that a Christian must be a man who responds to all these? A moment's reflection will clear this up. Have we not found in Christ meanings for moral life and character that are, not to many only, but to all of us, surrounded with the utmost practical difficulty? If it is difficult for some to respond to that intellectual meaning of Christ for faith which, for example, declares He is a God-man, it is also difficult for all to respond to that moral meaning of Christ for character which, for example, calls us to purity or love in life. Our responding to Christ, then, is an ideal. A perfect Christian would certainly respond to the complete meaning for thought and for life of the fact of Christ. Where is the perfect Christian? St. Paul counted not himself to have apprehended. Luther described himself as 'almost a Christian.'[1] A response may be real though not perfect. And here we must resist and even resent the strong but quite unjustified tendency to treat on different principles our moral and our intellectual response to Christ, and to mark a certain stage in specially the latter, to which a man who can be called a Christian must have advanced. There are those who will call a man Christian even though his practical response to the meanings of Christ for life be very meager, but will deny him the name if his intellectual response to the meanings of Christ for doctrinal belief be not

[1] *De Servo Arbitrio,* sect. clxviii.

very adequate. This is untenable. The amount of response to the meaning of Christ that is requisite to make a man a Christian is to be determined in the same way alike in matters of creed and matters of conduct. And if it be asked, then, how it is determined, the answer is clear. Men's mental and moral constitution and circumstances are so individual and so various, that no man can draw the line in this matter in either of its respects for another, nor can it be drawn for all men at once; but each man's responsibility, moral and intellectual, can be determined only in the region of the conscience, and therefore only by the Searcher of the conscience. 'The Lord knoweth them that are His.'

And now from all this we may come to a definition. If one were asked to state in terms what a Christian is, I should say something like this: a Christian is one who is responding to whatever meanings of Christ are, through God's spirit, being brought home to his intellectual or moral conscience. This is a definition at once exhaustive of the profoundest Christianity and admissive of the simplest. The meanings of Christ, either for thought or life, that one man may be able to respond to with intellectual assent or practical obedience, will be many and advanced; another man may, with equal earnestness and effort, be able, from his constitution, upbringing or circumstances, to respond to but the most elementary. Yet both are Christians if both are responding with a faithful conscience. One is a more mature Christian than the other, not, necessarily, a more real. Do not misunderstand me. I have not said, nor do I mean, that a man may respond to just that in Christ which he chooses; I spoke of what God's spirit brings home to the conscience, and that is quite another thing from the selection of our own inclination. Nor do I imply that it does not seriously matter how much meaning you put into Christ. It matters immensely. The Christian who has not something of the richness of the Christian faith as well as the victory of the Christian life is a great loser. But he is not 'lost.' He is to be encouraged, not excommunicated. It is not the amount of our achievement in either belief or conduct that Christ first looks at, but the honesty of our purpose. It is not the embarrassed following of Himself He blames, but the unfaithful. Where is the master more ready than He to take the will for the deed?

But we must spell this out a little more particularly. I have been speaking of a man's 'responding' to the meanings of Christ, and this expression requires some explanation. Well, to respond to the meanings of Christ is *to be* what one should and must be if these are really true. Let us recall the meanings of the fact of Christ we have been discussing—meanings for character, for faith, and for conscience—and then ask, 'What manner of persons ought we to be?' What love and trust and gratitude and obedience and service should ring and rule in our being? This is not anything vague or far away from life. It is life. Your being is just your life. The scenery, the surroundings, the furniture of your life are those of your being. All the affairs, interests, relations of your life contribute to make you what you are—to your being. Then it is in all these that you are to respond to Christ—to find out what bearings and directions the fact of Christ has for this fact of life and that, and to be true to them. In short, to be a Christian or—to use Dr. Chalmers's phrase—' to proceed ' upon Christianity is, day by day, in all the varied circumstances of experience within and without, to bring together and honestly relate to each other two great facts or sets of facts which, when so brought together, wonderfully elucidate and interpret one another—the fact of Christ and the facts of life.

Thus is Christianity concerned, not with merely a section of life—with the ' affairs of the soul '—but with all of it. No life—as I think Luther has said somewhere—is more worldly than a Christian's. It embraces everything that makes us what we are—all that, lived in a certain light and treated from a certain point of view. One of the great wrongs that ecclesiastical Christianity has done religion is to disparage or deny this, to give us the impression that a Christian life lived in the cloister is higher and holier than one lived in the family, the market, the secular arena of the world, and to bid us look to types of the former rather than the latter for saintship.[1] I cannot find any meaning such as this in the fact of Christ. The carpenter of Nazareth, who was among men 'eating and drinking'—He is 'our only Saint.' We must secularize saintship by sanctifying the secular life. 'What you do now even after the flesh,' says an early Father, 'that is spiritual, for in Christ Jesus you do everything.'[2] In that Christ Jesus, for it was by Him that all things were made, the Christian man can 'do everything'—except sin.

The exception, we all feel, is crucial. Whatever other meanings of Christ may be difficult to accept or disputable, this much is clear and cardinal—that the invitation and persuasion to be one with Him mean a war with sin. We know as an axiom that sin is something incon-

[1] While saying this, one must, too, recognize the value and even necessity of the ascetic ideal for certain periods of Christian history. As has been justly said (by, I suppose, the finest mind that Anglicanism has possessed since it lost the devout, subtle Newman) 'it must be looked upon as a great war, the only one that could have made any impression on the world of that day' (Dean Church's *Occasional Papers,* ii. 224). Christian morality, when fighting for its very life against the violent, savage grossness of the times, fought with a corresponding violence.

[2] Ignatius, *Ad* Ephes., viii.

sistent with Christ in its whole aim and principle and activity. Now we shall most assuredly not live life—this varied secular life—and yet avoid or overcome sin unless in addition to and, in a sense, over against all that has been said of the breadth and secularity of the religious life, we honestly admit another side of the question and observe, simply but really, two things.

One of these is prayer. Our Christianity is in constant danger of becoming merely a system—a doctrine or a praxis to which more or less faithfully we adhere. If it be but this, it certainly will not carry us victorious through the ceaseless, subtle and varied temptations to sin which meet us in life. There must be behind and in and through all this something personal. We must realize that Christ means that *God* is really and nearly taking to do with us, very authoritatively, very graciously, very wonderfully. Our religion must be less merely a doctrine to be studied and a duty to be done, than a call, a touch, an intercourse. Then is it a religion of a listening conscience, a wondering spirit, an awed soul, a loving and a contrite heart; and it is to these that sin is impotent. Now, all this ' mutual speaking and hearing between God and the soul '[1] finds its most real and most definite expression in that most simple and necessary thing, prayer. By it, as by hardly anything else, 'we come into God's presence and assure ourselves again of what He is in Himself and of what He is to us.'[2] No one, without that, is sin-proof. Of, on the other hand, the practical potency of prayer against sin little need be said. Take any known besetting sin in your life; pray against it. What is the result? The result is that they cannot live together. Your prayer will kill your sin, or your sin will kill your prayer. There is therefore no surer and clearer test of how a man is dealing with this crucial matter of sin in life than which, in especially his secret life, is the survivor—sin or prayer?

The other thing we must observe and admit is self-discipline or self-denial. I have asserted the breadth and worldliness of the Christian life—the life that responds to Christ. But a man will not go through the range of this rich and engrossing life saying 'Yes' to the meanings for it all of Christ without saying a

[1] Professor Candlish's *Christian Salvation*, p. 104.
[2] Professor Denney's *Gospel Questions and Answers*, p. 51.

'No' to many things. And this 'No' he must say, not only to what is plainly of sin, but also to much, at times at least, which cannot be so definitely characterized. The reason lies here. We have to work out our Christianity in the world with an imperfect and unreliable instrument. Theologians call it 'our fallen nature.' Well, whatever name you give to human nature, this, at least, is true of it—that it is very readily seduced by even morally legitimate things to another view and construction of life than Christ's. A man is simply either uncandid or unintelligent who does not admit this to be a real fact in the situation. This world is the place where men are to be Christians, but it is a place certainly where very easily they become not Christians; here is our true religious opportunity, but it is a perilous one. This is not a reason for fleeing from life. Such perils as come to a man in the path of his duty, he is meant to be ennobled by overcoming. But it is a reason for self-discipline and self-denial. What will imperil or deaden an honest and full response to Christ must be 'cut off.' This or that must be denied, and—what is perhaps more important—*all things* must be re-considered, re-valued, re-arranged in life. Some of us, for our own sakes or our neighbors', may have to do that more than others. Some may have, as Christ Himself plainly put it, to cut off their right hand or pluck out their right eye. It is not, as the mediæval church taught, the higher, more saintly ideal. It is, as Christ said, to 'enter the kingdom of Heaven maimed.' But in some way—and often the most real ways have, to others than a man himself, least appearance of being a self-denial at all—it must be done by all who would really mean to respond fully and faithfully to Christ in this complicated, compromising life. There is something singularly ennobling about the uncowled, unproclaimed self-discipline of a rich and passionate nature that loves life not the less but Christ the more. It can be done gladly if it be done for His sake, and some day He may very literally recompense it. That is the meaning of the lines:—

> 'Make me a cottage in the vale, she said,
>   Where I may mourn and pray;
> Yet pull not down my palace towers that are
>   So lightly, beautifully built;
> Perchance I may return with others there
>   When I have purged my guilt.'[1]

[1] Tennyson's *Palace of Art*.

The last couplet suggests another aspect of the meaning of Christ in life, and on it I add a word. The poet's lines suggest a larger future. Now, I have spoken of this life as the real sphere in the circumstances and conditions of which we must be Christians, and yet as a place in which our response to Christ is incomplete, imperiled, and to be maintained only by a warfare and with prayer and self-denial. At the end of life is the fact of death. That is a very great and real fact, so great and real a fact that any true or satisfying view of life must take account of death and have something to say about it. The fact of Christ does so. The ultimate meaning of Christ is a future meaning. He is He who not only 'was' in history and 'is' in experience, but 'is to come' in the beyond. Of that we know very little; it is one of those places where even the true religion hardly takes us out of agnosticism. But if Christ's meanings here for character, for faith, and for conscience are true promises, that meaning of Christ who is to come will be, than anything in this life, a 'far better.' It will be that if it lead from a good that is embarrassed, menaced, incomplete, to that good made safe, victorious, abundant, and yet not less but more real, personal and living. And so St. Paul, who said 'To me life is Christ' added 'and death gain.'

This may seem unnatural and strained, and yet I will say that there is nothing about Christianity that more convinces of its Divine devising than this, its suitability for both life here and life hereafter. It is thus that it declares itself to be the religion that men need. Christ is for life in the most real and secular sense. And we are for life in the most real and secular sense—we men to whom this life calls so stirringly and strongly and sweetly. But the more deeply and worthily we answer that call, is it not a call to something else? This life is richly, really good; but just in its very good—in truth or love or character or the service of man—are strange and subtle suggestions of a better than itself. 'I have found life,' said the subject of a modern biography,[1] 'sweet, bright, beautiful; I should dearly like to live it again.' Is this wish the true and deepest corollary to this experience? Is not the true and deepest thing in this life's sweetness, brightness, beauty, an intimation, a glimpse, an earnest of something

[1] *Life of Fitzjames Stephen.*

sweeter, brighter, yet more beautiful? Is it not this which gives to our actions their tenderest tints, to our affections their purest pathos, and informs even nature with that subtle significance which makes us say that

> 'the meanest flower that blows can give
> Thoughts that do often lie too deep for tears.'[1]

The sea of the Infinite laps upon the shore of the finite where we now live. When we sigh for satisfaction here, we do not realize that in this world satisfaction is for us a form of suicide. We are made for this life, yet not for this life only, but, after this, for a 'far better.' And so is our Christianity. The Christ who disclosed such fit meanings for us in the discipline of our life here, discloses a like fittedness for our nature when the last chapter of that discipline comes and we look out to the future. Thus a Christian man blesses God every day of his life, and, on the greatest day of a man's life, which is the day of his death, blesses Him still and not fearfully or repiningly enters into the untold meanings of the endless fact of Christ.

I must close, but would at least mention one question out of many that remain. We have

[1] Wordsworth, *Intimations of Immortality*.

been speaking of what it is to be a Christian. But why be a Christian?

There are two voices neither of which is ever long silent in the heart of any serious and honest-thinking man. One is a voice within that speaks to a man of himself. It shuts the door on the throng of the world, in which so easily we forget our personal responsibilities and even our own moral identity, and confers with us *solus cum solo* about our individual character and destiny. It is a small voice, never overheard in another, easily drowned even in oneself. But whenever there is a stillness in our life—especially if the great silence has hushed our spirits by its nearness—it speaks out clear and makes us listen. The other is not a small voice. It is the multitudinous murmur of humanity in its labor and sorrow—now an uncouth roar as of the breaking sea, now a moan as of the homeless wind. This, too, can be drowned by a selfishness, even a religious selfishness, that dulls the ears and deadens the heart, but again and again it disturbs men and awakens within them thoughts of a worthier life than that lived but for themselves. These are the two great voices that are ever speaking to the human heart. They are two voices, yet they bear but one message. They are both a call to look to and to learn of Jesus Christ. We need Him for our own sakes if we are going to live rightly and die restfully; we need Him for others' sakes if in any deep and real way we would serve them. Alike by every reason of regard towards our true selves and every call of love towards our brother, we are bound to be Christians. And ah! there is this too, if only we will think of it and can read it as it is written over our lives and in the fact of Christ —the unmeasured and unmerited goodness and grace that God has shown to you and me.

These are reasons for being a Christian. They sum themselves up in this. Jesus said of Himself, ' I am the Truth.' In these lectures I have not argued from the authority of Church or Bible; I have tried to state Christ, who, if He be the Truth, is His own authority. Does He not mean to heart or mind or conscience *some* things that are deeply and really truth? Then, to be a Christian is the first principle of a true life.